SACRED MEMORIES

The Civil War Monument Movement in Texas

By Kelly McMichael

Texas State Historical Association
Denton

Library of Congress Cataloging-in-Publication Data

McMichael, Kelly.

Number nineteen in the Fred Rider Cotton Popular History Series.

Published by the Texas State Historical Association.
Design by David Timmons.
Frontispiece: Confederate Monument in Denton. Photo by the author.

CONTENTS

East Texas

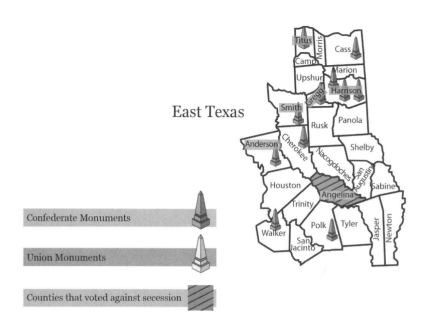

Confederate Monuments

Union Monuments

Counties that voted against secession

North Texas

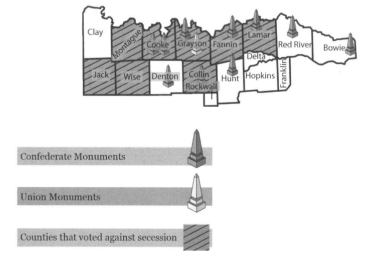

Confederate Monuments

Union Monuments

Counties that voted against secession

North Central
Texas

Parker | Tarrant | Dallas | Rains | Wood
Kaufman | Van Zandt
Hood | Johnson | Ellis | Henderson
Hill | Navarro

 Confederate Monuments

Union Monuments

Counties that voted against secession

Central Texas

McLennan | Falls | Bell | Burnet | Llano | Williamson | Travis | Bastrop

 Confederate Monuments

 Union Monuments

 Counties that voted against secession

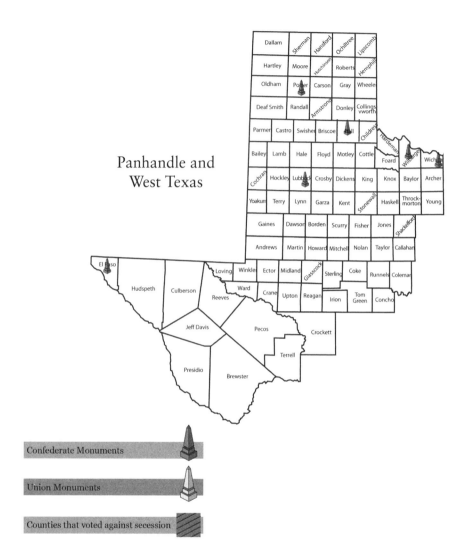

Panhandle and
West Texas

Confederate Monuments

Union Monuments

Counties that voted against secession

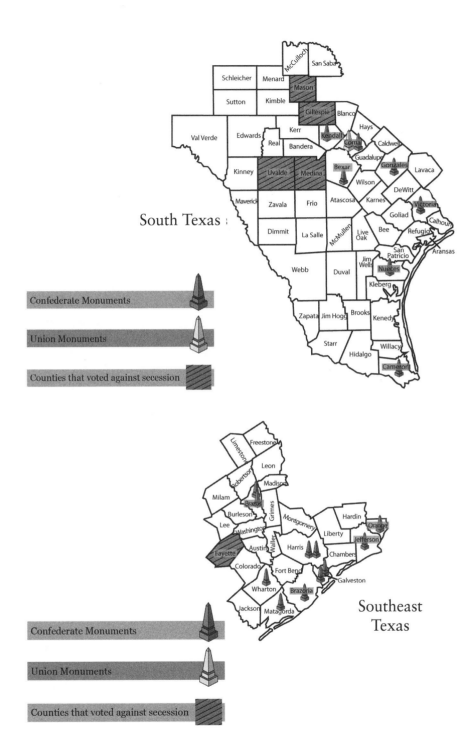

South Texas

Confederate Monuments

Union Monuments

Counties that voted against secession

Southeast Texas

Confederate Monuments

Union Monuments

Counties that voted against secession

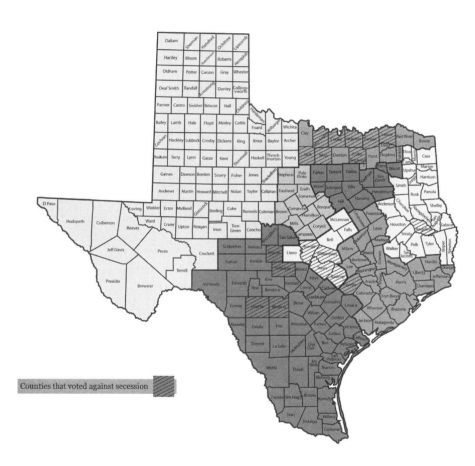

Counties that voted against secession

Introduction

THE CHILDREN'S VOICES ECHOED through the tall canopy of oaks that surrounded the courthouse, their laughter giving them away in a game of hide-and-seek. One child counted, eyes turned into the bark of an old tree. Another poised silently behind a large cannon and a third crept as quietly as possible in her long dress and stiff black shoes behind the Civil War monument in the center of the lawn.

The adults who had gathered nearby were chatting, most commenting on the clear, calm weather—always uncertain in North Central Texas in March—and preparing for the day's celebration. The men, growing overly warm in their gray woolen military uniforms, hung the last of the bunting and crepe paper and planted the Confederate and United States flags around the square. The ladies' hoopskirts and crinoline crackled in the air as they placed a few chairs around the monument for the elderly among the expected crowd.

As it turned out, seventy-five men, women, and children gathered that day in March 1996 in period dress to rededicate the city of Sherman's one-hundred-year-old Confederate monument. The parents quieted their children while Mark Farrington, commander of the Colonel Reeves Eleventh Texas Cavalry Camp 349, Sons of Confederate Veterans (SCV), explained to those present that "we are here today not to honor the war, but the warriors." The memorial, originally unveiled on April 22, 1897, by the Sherman Chapter of the United Daughters of the Confederacy (UDC), remained a site of memory, despite the passing of the years.[1]

1

The Sherman UDC intended their monument to serve as a physical memory, the very presence of which, so prominently placed downtown in the middle of the legal and business district, would constantly recall the war. Not willing to leave that memory in doubt, the Daughters stated their objective clearly in the inscription:

> sacred to the memory of your Confederate dead,
> true patriots, they fought for home and country, for
> the holy principles of self-government—the only true liberty
> their sublime self-sacrifices and unsurpassed valor
> will teach future generations the lesson of high born
> patriotism, of devotion to duty, of exalted courage,
> of southern chivalry.

Sherman's monument would demonstrate the characteristics and values the Daughters held in esteem. The town's children, hiding behind the monument in a simple game, would absorb the ideals of patriotism, duty, and courage.[2]

The sixty-eight large, public-initiated monuments to the Civil War in Texas seem to be bound in a collective narrative—a public memory that speaks of the great chasm of the Civil War, of a nation rocked to its very foundation, torn apart by differences so great that the blood-letting that ensued was inevitable. But are these great stone and bronze memorials really bound by a single memory? Do they represent only a single narrative? This book tells the story of these monuments, of the Texans who erected them, and their reasons for raising large sums of money to purchase memorials to honor the Confederacy and the Union.[3]

War memorials are fundamentally public art, but art imbued with a political and cultural purpose. Yes, the people who erected them intended for their aesthetic appeal to be appreciated, but by their very nature, monuments dedicated to commemorate a war are expected to convey a message.

In our own time, the Vietnam War memorial in Washington, D.C., illustrates a monument's ability to carry profound meaning. Simple, sleek, and barely visible until one is upon the wall, the memorial, created by funds collected from citizens but placed on public ground (like most of Texas's Civil War monuments), on first glance seems to have no overt message. There is no symbolic statuary, no poetic inscription, just the long continuous march of the names of the dead and the objects that observers have added. And it is in this simplicity that the monument seems to convey its message of homage to the countless men and women who died but have not been forgotten. The notes, flowers, combat boots, and other items left by friends and families form an interactive testament with the monument of an enduring legacy.[4]

This monument has become a sacred shrine for many families, a physical location where memories take form. It is sometimes difficult to compare Civil War monuments with this single commemoration. After all, hundreds of towns across the United States have memorials to the Civil War, many strikingly similar in appearance. In an age of easy transport and sprawling cities, their sheer abundance and placement has rendered them meaningless. Citizens pass them on the street without a second glance: the ubiquitous soldier statue on the courthouse lawn. Texans placed many of the monuments in the heart of downtown districts, public spaces where commerce once reigned, replaced now by boarded-over shop windows and empty sidewalks. These monuments have fallen into disrepair, mostly ignored. Perhaps at the time they were built, though, citizens felt an emotional grounding to them akin to the feelings evoked for many by the Vietnam memorial. Though made of stone, monuments are receptacles of emotion.

When a war memorial is erected, the stakes are always high. Who erects the memorial and why they do so are vital questions because monuments do more than just carry emotions; they represent cultural power. Not only do statues serve to remind an individual of his or her own lived experience of an event, but the memorial creators intend them to carry a message to future generations. Monuments and the process of choosing, fundraising, building, and unveiling provide a select group with the opportunity to shape society's memory of an event or individual—a potentially powerful position within a community.[5]

War memorials serve as a means of unifying a community's collective memory. They are tangible representations that bring meaning, understanding, or closure to a people, creating a single, collective experience for the group. The creation of collective memory is not just a simple act of recalling the past, but an intricately contrived means of forming a particular social identity based on a largely invented story. Creating and controlling a group's shared memory constitutes real societal power.[6]

It is little wonder, then, that the people who erected Texas's Civil War monuments charged them with the power to represent their social and political interests. The vast majority of the state's monuments honor the Confederacy. Texans, along with citizens from six other Southern states, voted to secede in the spring of 1861 following Abraham Lincoln's election to the presidency. Though several powerful men in the state, including Governor Sam Houston, argued against disunion, the majority of citizens, representing 104 out of the state's 122 organized counties, voted to leave the Union.[7]

Why did Texas join the Confederacy? Many explanations abound, including the abstract idea that the federal government threatened states' rights, but the legislative convention called to discuss secession in Texas in 1861 wrote in its "Declaration of the Causes which Impel the State of Texas to Secede from the Federal Union" that the "great sectional party" of Lincoln was hostile to the "beneficent and patriarchal system of African slavery." The delegates argued primarily that Texas seceded to defend its interests—chief among those interests was the perpetuation of slavery.[8]

But four years and 620,000 deaths later the war's meaning and purpose began to be doubted. Stumbling through the federal government's Reconstruction policies, Texans and other Southerners attempted to make sense of the decisions they had made and justify their actions. The myth of the Lost Cause emerged during this period. Evolving out of defeat, dislocation, and desperation, the myth attempted to explain the war and quickly came to represent one of the dominant collective memories in the South. The Lost Cause became a collective tradition, claiming that secession was just and legal and that the war represented a contest in which both sides had been in the right. The South argued that it fought for the constitutional principle of self-determination and the preservation of the homeland, claiming that the region lost because of overwhelming Northern numbers, not Southern shortcomings. With slavery legally ended, the Lost Cause marginalized and romanticized the peculiar institution.[9]

The monuments Texans erected to the Confederacy perpetuated

these romanticized memories of the war. And though the majority of the statues erected in the state glorified the South's cause, three of the monuments represented a potential counter-memory. These three memorials provide a Unionist interpretation of the war's meaning, rationalized by claims that the North fought to keep the Union together and to maintain the integrity of the Constitution. The monuments to the Union in the state memorialize the men who sacrificed for the United States' perpetuation, honoring their patriotism and giving meaning to their deaths. Texans erected these three monuments to celebrate individuals or small groups of individuals. They include the *Treue Der Union* monument in Comfort, a granite figure of a United States soldier in the Fairview Cemetery in Denison, and the Civil War monument in New Braunfels. The monument in New Braunfels is especially interesting because it was dedicated to the men who died in the war, in both the North and South. Representing in some sense the community's reconciliatory attitude, the town inscribed the statue to "the memory of our fallen soldiers."[10]

Perhaps more compelling than this counter-memory is the forgetting that both Southern and Northern monuments allowed. While on the one hand they represented a vindication of the South's cause and a glorification of the North's victory, the monuments also signified a form of social amnesia. Where was the memory of slavery or of emancipation? No monument erected in the state carried any sign or symbol of the 400,000 slaves freed by the war. For more than twenty years several groups spoke of creating a national "faithful slave" monument to memorialize the institution. Only two such statues exist in the South, one erected in Fort Mill, South Carolina (1896), and the other in Natchitoches, Louisiana (1927). Both were dedicated to the faithful field hands and mammies, in highly romanticized expression, who remained working on the plantations after the war. These memorials reflected the sentimental story of benevolent slavery that whites constructed. But any monument about slavery, even one to faithful slaves, proved too controversial to gain widespread acceptance and no national monument was erected that celebrated the contributions of slavery to the landscape or economy.[11]

The Texans who erected Civil War monuments had a clear vision of what they wanted future generations to remember about the war. The message is not surprising—the majority of the monuments were unveiled between 1893 and 1910, a period marked by a severe depression, social unrest, the rise of Populism, mass immigration, urbanization, industrialization, imperialism, lynching, and Jim Crow laws. Society was in turmoil, and uncertainty loomed around every corner. A monument might anchor a community against social and political doubt. Erected by the white political and civic leaders of a town (and white Texans unveiled all of the state's Civil War monuments), the memorials and the ceremonies that accompanied them reassured citizens. The monuments sent a message of white supremacy, of community solidarity, of the importance of the average man. Town after town erected statues that portrayed the common soldier, most in uniform with a gun carried casually in hand. These images represented a cult of sacrifice composed of white Southerners, no matter their station in life, united by color and fighting for a common cause.[12]

While these monuments may have carried a shared message about the war's meaning, the men and women who funded and erected them had other agendas for the monuments besides just broadcasting a specific war interpretation. Civil War monuments also represented a complicated negotiation of gender roles. Tensions rose between men and women, who often erected memorials for different purposes.

Men, always veterans and usually members of the United Confederate Veterans Association (UCV), erected a minority of the state's monuments. Old soldiers established the UCV in 1889 as a benevolent, historical, social, and literary society. Its organizers planned to unite, in a general federation, all of the varied associations of Southern veterans. There were several active veterans' organizations at this time in Texas, each formed independently around a specific military regiment or unit. For example, both Terry's Texas Rangers (Eighth Texas Cavalry) and Hood's Brigade (Fourth Texas Infantry) formed postwar associations, met annually for reunions, and eventually sponsored monuments. The UCV offered a larger, regional umbrella for these independent groups, and many veterans responded enthusiastically to the new organization. Total membership in the UCV probably approached 160,000, or about 25 percent of the Southern soldiers who survived the war. The percentage of members in Texas was even higher. Of an estimated 18,000 to 27,000 living veterans in Texas in

1890, more than 9,000 joined the two hundred fifty-five UCV camps in the state. The organization remained active into the mid-1940s and a few of these camps erected large memorials to their comrades. For example, the Richard Taylor Camp, UCV, erected the monument in Jefferson, meeting part of their goal to preserve and cherish their service record.[13]

Although many veterans' sons donated money to their fathers' monuments, most of the sons had little interest in building memorials. The younger men, now the business and political leaders and backbone of the local economy, simply were more interested in making money and getting on with the future than with living in the past. If they did support a monument, it was because its unveiling furthered their own commercial interests. For example, local businesses owned by men sponsored the dedication parade and ceremony of Sherman's memorial unveiling ceremony in 1897, and more than 5,000 people descended on the small town for the celebration, many taking rooms in the town's hotels, eating in restaurants, and making purchases in stores. An unveiling gave the town fathers a chance to highlight their community, and area Chambers of Commerce predicted that land sales in the area would increase afterward as visitors, welcomed to a beautiful and progressive city, saw the town's advantages.[14]

Charles B. Emanuel, a speaker at the Rusk Confederate Reunion in 1901, summarized men's attitudes toward monument building in the speech he delivered. Emanuel argued that men's work ended with the war, and the next task, that of "preserving the memories of the gallant heroes who fell in defense of our native land," was left to the women. In other words, Texas's men had moved on and were engaged in more profitable, and in their opinion, more important matters—such as rebuilding the region and making money. If men became involved, explained J. W. Graves in the *Houston Chronicle* in 1909, it was because as "commercial men, even putting the question on its lowest plane, we believe that our commercial prestige would be enhanced and our material standing elevated in the minds of the whole world by an exemplification of finer feeling and nobler sentiments, as such a movement [to build a Texas monument at Vicksburg, Mississippi] would prove." Memorial work, while appreciated by citizens, was not of primary importance and because men gave it such a low priority, the task of memorializing the Confederacy could be and was taken up by women.[15]

Though veterans erected a few of Texas's monuments, women, all members of the United Daughters of the Confederacy, erected the majority. Some people at the time questioned why the daughters and not the sons chose to spend their time building memorials. As Texas UDC member Kate Alma Orgain of Temple explained, "[I]t is natural and appropriate that women should engage in commemorative work. When death comes to our homes and takes the loved ones, it is the woman, the wife, the mother who lays away the old worn hat, the baby slipper, the broken toy. It is women who keep the grave and cultivate the flowers around it."[16]

The women of the Texas Division of the United Daughters of the Confederacy had been "keeping the grave" since the state division formed in 1896. In the national UDC, an organization that attracted members from all fifty states and a few foreign countries, Texas consistently registered more chapters and more members than any other state. The Daughters claimed that their objectives were "memorial, benevolent, historical, and social," and the association proposed to "fulfill duties of sacred charity toward Confederate veterans and their descendents." Membership was based on heredity: the widows, wives, mothers, sisters, nieces, and lineal descendants of those who served or gave material aid could join, as could women and their lineal descendants who had helped the Confederacy and its soldiers in some verifiable way during the war.[17]

UDC members, unlike their male peers, embraced the work and were empowered by their ability to raise funds to create monuments when others had given up. Some men may have seen only the commercial prospects in monument building, but the Daughters saw Confederate memorials as one of the best means to remind Texans of their obligations and duties as citizens. The UDC believed that each time an individual passed a lone soldier cast in marble on a courthouse lawn, paused to admire a granite obelisk, or hid behind a memorial in a game of hide-and-go-seek, he or she would comprehend and internalize the beliefs and values the organization associated with the Old South. Such assimilation would, according to the Daughters, encourage correct social order by stressing patriotism, duty, and resignation. Not only did these monuments offer a history lesson to Texans, but their unveilings provided the Daughters with a chance to focus public attention on women. UDC chapters seized every possible opportunity to promote and emphasize Southern women's strength and independence. Though the Daughters would have as difficult a time raising funds as had the veterans, they, unlike the old soldiers, never gave up. The Daughters proved better fundraisers than the men; they had more free time and believed that they had more to lose if a monument was not erected and more to gain if it was.

Many of these women believed that their husbands were too preoccupied with material interests, certainly evident in the men's unwillingness to initiate monument construction, and that male attitudes had led to the decline in personalism so rampant in the quickly urbanizing Southern society. Many UDC members believed that their biological roles in life—as wives and mothers—lent them insight into the inner soul, an insight that gave women special permission to express positive morals and virtues. The Daughters endowed their monuments with words and images meant to represent the values they believed lacking in society, values like sacrifice and patriotism.

Monuments gave these women an opportunity to project the morals they valued, but they provided them with other opportunities and other messages as well. UDC members believed that their mothers had worked in complementary roles with their fathers during the Civil War—positions that had been absolutely essential to the region's cause, and they wanted their mothers' efforts to be remembered. Much of women's monument work in Texas attempted to guarantee that women were recognized and remembered for their efforts during the war and its aftermath. For example, the inscription on the monument in Gainesville reads, "to the women of the Confederacy, whose pious ministrations to our wounded soldiers and sailors soothed the last hours of those who died far from the objects of their tenderest love; and whose patriotism will teach their children to emulate the deeds of their revolutionary sires." In one inscription, Gainesville's UDC chapter established the importance of women's participation in the Civil War and validity as instructors of patriotism.[18]

But the monuments and the unveiling ceremonies did more for Texas women than just project values and honor their mothers—the job of erecting memorials helped to expand women's traditional role in society. The Daughters planned huge fundraisers and elaborate celebrations with little help or influence from their men, ensuring themselves a form of work and independence and a prominent and vocal place in their communities. Not content to work in the shadows, the UDC frequently chose its own members to speak alongside more obvious speakers (local judges, state senators, and even governors) at the unveilings; women stood proudly in front of mixed-gender audiences and expressed their thoughts and opinions. While some of the ladies remained demurely behind the long banquet tables passing out food, others chose to stand on the podiums—defying the image of Southern women as quiet, acquiescing "belles."

One of the Daughters's first attempts to erect a state monument reflects both the public's general lack of interest in Confederate monuments and the UDC's desire to build them despite that lack of interest. Though the monument drive was riddled with setbacks, the Daughters eventually succeeded. When they did, the women of the Texas UDC realized that they could gain power and prestige for themselves with such projects.

The Albert Sidney Johnston Chapter of the UDC was organized in Austin in 1897 and reported that their "grand objective" was to "erect a monument over the grave of Albert Sidney Johnston, that gallant commander, who when dying, begged that his body might be laid to rest in Texas soil." The chapter soon realized that it could not raise sufficient funds to create a fitting tribute. That same year, the state secretary of the UDC, Sarah Fontaine Sampson, said that she knew "every chapter in the state is probably contemplating the erection of a monument," but that it would be wiser for the organization to "unite their efforts and produce one great work, that of the Albert Sidney Johnston monument in Austin." This proposal was brought before the division at the 1897 convention, but the ladies did not even consider it. Although most of the Daughters preferred to work toward the raising of monuments in their local areas, the Texas Division's president, Benedette Tobin, agreed with Sampson that a single great monument would better represent the state than several smaller ones.[19]

President Tobin and the Albert Sidney Johnston Chapter of Austin began in earnest to raise the funds necessary to create a monument.

Tobin organized a monument committee of thirty-four women, who then presented a petition to the regular session of the Texas legislature in 1898 asking for a state appropriation to build the monument. The legislature denied the UDC's petition. Tobin then increased the committee to fifty women and asked Senator R. N. Stafford of Mineola for suggestions and advice. Though Tobin died in 1900, her successor, Eliza Sophia Johnson, continued to pressure the state for money to build an Albert Sidney Johnston monument. Following Stafford's instructions, Johnson organized a media campaign to influence the state legislature. She and the UDC monument committee sent a copy of the petition to all the leading daily newspapers in the state. They also mailed 2,600 copies of the petition to prominent men in the state with a personal letter asking each of them to sign the petition and return it to the governor. The committee sent an additional two hundred copies to all the United Confederate Veterans camps in Texas. The UDC tried again in 1901 to secure an appropriation at the state legislature's regular session but failed. Not discouraged, Johnson made one more attempt. She sent two hundred circulars and personal letters to all of Texas's legislators and wrote to every newspaper in the state seeking support. Finally, at a special session of the legislature in the autumn of 1901, she brought the petition before the House once more, and "after having first aroused a healthy sentiment over the state for its passage," received a $10,000 appropriation.[20]

The UDC had succeeded in building a state Confederate monument, but by eliciting help from the state of Texas, the Daughters sacrificed control of the monument. The legislature organized a committee to direct the monument's construction, and while Johnson served on the committee, she was the only UDC representative to do so. Still, the Daughters considered the monument's completion a success, and many of the women realized that they could potentially wield great power by banding together and applying pressure on state or local governments and local newspapers.[21]

Despite this initial success, Texans continued to find it difficult to collect the money needed to build monuments. Public donations funded most of the state's monuments, and even when men initiated the memorial, women generally did the fundraising. It sometimes took years to collect the large amounts needed. Dallas's UDC chapter managed to raise the funds needed in only three years, but the ladies of Huntsville spent fifty-seven years trying to gather enough money to erect a small granite marker. The economy in Texas, while stronger than elsewhere in the South, was still stagnant, and those citizens who had money were reluctant to part with it for the building of a memorial. There were always other things more crucial to purchase—a new plow, screens for the windows, food for the table, shoes for the children.[22]

The women who raised the funds for monuments came mostly from the upper and middle classes, but they tried to appeal to the sensibilities of all white Texans. They found that simply asking for donations rarely resulted in more than a few dollars. Sometimes the local veterans' camp might pull together and come up with a $50 or $100 contribution, but that still left thousands of needed dollars. So the Daughters became creative. They sponsored musical evenings of song and dance (charging admission) and sold tea, ice cream, and cakes. They hosted fiddlers' contests, bake sales, rummage sales, and worked as sales clerks at local businesses for a percentage of the profit. They solicited funds from local stores and requested a percentage of the admission prices to state and county fairs. They pinched and hoarded and held penny drives at their children's schools. Sometimes they approached the state. The UDC pressured the state legislature to appropriate monies on more than one occasion, a mission that proved long and not always successful.[23]

By sheer determination, the women erected their statues. Once the memorials were in place, the Daughters, veterans, and town leaders organized huge parades and unveiling ceremonies to celebrate. The monument dedication in Dallas in 1897 gathered an estimated 40,000 people and included a parade, "love feast," banquets, and a ball. The Llano Daughters brought in the governor to speak in 1916—a rare treat for rural Texans who rarely encountered the great men of the state.[24]

It is odd that Llano's Daughters waited so many years after the war to erect a memorial, not because the citizens of Llano were more patriotic or wealthier than others, but because the small community had become, by the early 1900s, the largest granite distribution area in the state. Although the largest and wealthiest monument dealer in the

South was the McNeel Marble Company of Marietta, Georgia, Texas had its own marble dealer who made an enormous amount of money producing and selling Confederate monuments. Sculptor and stonecutter Frank Teich was born in Germany in 1856. Trained and apprenticed in Europe, Teich immigrated to the United States in 1878 and worked in several states on various projects. In 1883 he became superintendent of granite cutters working on the Texas state capitol, liked Texas, and decided to stay.[25]

Two years later, Teich opened a marble yard on the present site of the Medical Arts Building in San Antonio, across from the Alamo. His company did much of the fancy stonework in San Antonio, including the Kampman Building and City Hall, but Teich found his health failing and sought a more comfortable climate. Relocating to the Hill Country, Teich discovered a granite vein in Llano County and opened Teich Monumental Works, two miles from the city of Llano. Known as the father of the Texas granite industry, Teich was a good salesman but made many enemies.[26]

One of his enemies and his toughest competitor was Pompeo Coppini. The Italian-born sculptor did not start as an enemy; in fact, Coppini had answered a newspaper advertisement placed by Teich, who was looking for a sculptor to complete a Confederate monument. Teich hired Coppini to finish a statue of Jefferson Davis, the last figure to be completed of four that would adorn the memorial to Hood's Brigade in Austin. The recent immigrant did such fine work that the veterans demanded that Teich scrap the other three busts and have Coppini make all the figures. The two men fell out over the monument.[27]

Angry with Teich, Coppini struck out on his own, and monument commissions soon followed. One of his best known sculptures is the *Littlefield Fountain Memorial* on the campus of the University of Texas at Austin. In addition to numerous Confederate statues, Coppini also produced the Sam Houston monument at Huntsville and a group statue called *The Victims of the Galveston Flood*, given to the University of Texas at Austin.

The monument business fostered a large industry in the state, and UDC chapters and their cities vied to see who could raise the largest and most impressive monuments, a competition fueled by aggressive dealers who used sentimental language to encourage the building of even more monuments. Coppini wrote extensively about the commercialism that sprang up around the building of Confederate monuments. He complained that "it is easy to influence small communities to give parks or other utilitarian projects for memorials, as the small masses are not educated to art appreciation." Coppini added that some unscrupulous men appealed to the Confederates "with sentimental hypocritical devotion to their cause, that as the Confederate Army wore the gray uniforms, their Memorials should therefore be built of gray granite, even if it came from Yankee states to make Yankee manufacturing rich."[28]

But Coppini saved his most scathing remarks for the father of Texas's granite industry. Coppini claimed that Teich was responsible for developing the gray granite industry in the state because he had "worked that gag [building monuments out of Confederate gray] with the Confederates and the State politicians for all it was worth and with a handsome profit." Teich could "talk the language of those that know nothing of the value of the thing they were to buy," claimed Coppini, "by misrepresenting himself as something he never was." Coppini wrote that Teich was responsible for the "lowgrade commercial distribution of shameful public monument monstrosities" in the state.[29]

Certainly from an artistic standpoint, Coppini's monuments are more sophisticated than those produced by Teich. (Coppini's *The Last Stand*, in Victoria, is a stunning piece of statuary unlike any other in the state.) But many UDC chapters chose to buy mass-produced memorials rather than wait five, ten, or even fifteen years trying to raise enough money to hire a sculptor of Coppini's quality. Fort Worth's Julia Jackson Chapter of the UDC contacted Coppini in 1921 to request a catalog of designs ranging from five to twenty thousand dollars. The sculptor sniffed that "artists have no catalogs because each monument is individually made." Coppini claimed he would meet with the Fort Worth chapter and discuss plans, but he could not "compete with the cold blooded and mercenary stone dealers, who love no art and build monuments simply to sell stones." The UDC in Fort Worth could never raise sufficient funds for such an ambitious project. In 1938 they placed a small stone on the courthouse lawn to honor the Confederacy.[30] Coppini's complaints reflect the unplanned nature of Civil War commemoration in the state. Monuments were always born locally, and no central commissions on art or state boards regulated the selection or construction of the memorials. Even those placed on the capitol grounds failed to fall under a single committee that might unify their style or suggest artistic placement. The monuments erected in Texas were reflections of the towns that unveiled them, mirroring the community's perception of its place in history and sense of itself economically and culturally compared to neighboring towns. Those communities that found historical continuity in a Civil War past erected monuments to the sectional strife, while other towns (for example, Giddings, Gonzales, and La Grange), linked themselves in time more with the Texas Revolution and erected memorials to the Texas heroes of 1836.

This need to connect to a historic past that manifested itself among communities helps explain the seeming incongruence of county seats like Cooke, Lamar, Collin, Bastrop, and Williamson raising monuments to the Confederacy. These counties had voted "no" to secession, yet their citizens later built Civil War monuments. The memorials honored the men and women of the war generation, not the war itself. The memorials helped explain the historical past of the community—a community that might not have initially agreed with secession but sent men to fight and die for the Confederacy during the war.

Texas towns attempted to connect with a historical past throughout the late 1890s and early 1900s partly to create a sense of belonging during a period of rapid upheaval, but also as part of the larger City Beautiful movement that ignited across the United States during those years. Proponents of the movement believed that by making the physical landscapes of their cities beautiful, they could emphasize or instruct citizens in specific civic virtues and values. The erection of monuments proved one of the easiest means of combining these themes: beautification, civic lessons, and social cohesion.[31]

Certainly many Texas women, including those in the United Daughters of the Confederacy, were familiar with the ideas of the City Beautiful movement. Katie Cabell Currie Muse, the mother of the UDC in Texas and the division's first president, traveled to Chicago in 1893 and toured the World's Columbian Exposition and Fair—an entirely planned industrial town called the "white city" that had been created

15

on the principles of the City Beautiful ideals. This tour, combined with her initial reason for being in Chicago—the erection of a Confederate monument to the men who had died at Camp Douglas, a Union prisoner-of-war camp—inspired Muse. She returned home to Dallas and made plans to create a woman's club that would agitate for the beautification and moral uplifting of the state. She started the UDC and immediately went to work encouraging the building of monuments that would commemorate the Civil War and add an artistic and virtuous aspect to city landscapes.[32]

Monument construction enabled many Daughters to break out of their stereotyped roles in Southern society, but the movement made no such allowances for Texas's African Americans. Although there is no record of African Americans participating officially in any of the monument ceremonies, black Texans expressed their opinions, often in unspoken ways. For example, a black woman hurled a rock at one of the parade carriages carrying UDC members at the Dallas monument unveiling in 1897. While the newspaper only reported the woman's actions and not her words, a rock crashing into a buggy of well-dressed Daughters clearly expressed the African American's opinion of the ladies' ceremony.[33]

Texas's German Americans fared better after the Civil War than did African Americans. They were, of course, white, and despite the fact that many Germans had remained loyal to the Union during the conflict, white Texans rallied together after the war, more interested in economic prosperity and the separation of the races than former ideological differences. German Americans in the community of Comfort, in the middle of the Hill Country, dedicated the first of two monuments in the state specifically to the Union in August 1866. The *Treue Der Union* monument may well be the first memorial in the South dedicated to the United States after the Civil War. The obelisk honored the sacrifice of an estimated thirty-six German Texans who died at the hands of Confederate soldiers in the Battle of the Nueces on August 10, 1862.[34]

Local Daughters erected the first Confederate monument in Texas in Waco's Oakwood Cemetery on May 2, 1893, the day set aside as Decoration Day (now called Memorial Day). Coming together with area veterans in the center of the state, the UDC placed flowers on graves and sang hymns on the grounds of the memorial. Twenty-six years after the first Union monument had been erected in Texas in Comfort, citizens honored the Confederacy through statuary.[35]

Texas did not lag far behind the other former Confederate states in erecting statues. White Southerners across the region had found it difficult to build monuments in the immediate years after the war. In Richmond, Virginia's veterans and Daughters erected the first large, public memorial to the Confederacy in 1875. Ten years later the cities of Montgomery, Alabama, Atlanta, Georgia, and Savannah, Georgia, also erected monuments, but it was not until the 1890s that memorials became widespread and common throughout the region.[36]

Like Civil War monuments across the country, the early memorials in Texas were funerary in nature. Both the monuments in Comfort and Waco honored and remembered the dead. One was erected in a cemetery and the other became a cemetery site because the bones of the Comfort men were buried alongside the monument. These early memorials represented the need to grieve and the need to mark the graves of those lost. They were less political and social in nature and were meant to be markers of a sacred history.

Of the sixty-eight monuments erected in Texas, thirty-two were unveiled between 1900 and 1915, the most active period of monument construction in the state. Of those thirty-two, thirty were built on or were later moved to the lawns of courthouses. Though a few of Texas's towns placed shafts in their cemeteries, most wanted their visible symbols of memory displayed in more conspicuous and more useful locations: in city parks or the grounds of county courthouses. Almost all of the monuments in the state are of two types: either a smooth obelisk or a Confederate soldier atop a column.

Why did Texans wait to erect the majority of its Civil War monuments forty years after the war had ended? A host of factors likely played a role in the long gap between the end of the war and the dedication of the monuments. Though not as war-torn as many states, Texas still suffered economically and citizens concentrated on grieving for the dead and rebuilding their lives. Money was scarce and other priorities were more pressing. Though the dead were lovingly remembered in homes and on Decoration Day, Texans must have known the political uncertainties they faced initially as Reconstruction took shape and new governments formed. Would it have been right and appropriate for the vanquished to erect monuments to their own defeat immediately after the war? The South needed time to absorb and find meaning in its loss before it was ready to honor it in a public fashion.[37]

Well over a century has passed since Texans erected the first of these Civil War monuments. The monuments are arranged in this book by physical location rather than chronologically or ideologically, with Texas divided into seven regions based roughly on geographical and historical ties. There are monuments to the war throughout the state, although the majority are concentrated in the eastern two-thirds—the area of Texas most similar to the rest of the South. This area, encompassing all of East, North, North Central, and Central Texas, developed economically much like the rest of the South. The people who settled Texas's eastern half hailed from Southern states and brought with them a predilection for an agriculturally based economy, particularly the growing of corn and cotton, and more important in terms of the eventual war, slavery.

But, perhaps surprisingly, people in the western half of Texas erected monuments to the Civil War, too. Although the area has long been considered more Western than Southern, cities throughout the Panhandle and South Texas commemorated the Civil War through statuary. These people might have earned their living by ranching, market gardening, or fruit growing, but they were essentially Southern by heritage and by birth, and their attempts to honor their local veterans (usually Confederate veterans), reflected this.[38]

Whether placed in a cemetery or park or on a courthouse lawn, each monument tells its own story. It represents the lives of its creators as much as it does the Civil War generation it is meant to commemorate. Through the years, the marble and granite pillars have formed a memory, but a memory that has been marked by the changes of time. The Civil War monuments stand today as tokens of a war fought to define the Constitution and the meaning of citizenship in a democratic nation, one side attempting to expand that definition, the other limiting it. They also represent the oppression of white supremacy, forever reminding us that freedom must prevail.

Beyond the ideology, the monuments remind us of the individual men and women caught up in the fire of the war—of masters and slaves, of Northern farmers turned soldiers, and Southern women fleeing to Texas to escape Sherman's troops. They represent the human element of the war and ultimately, that is what their creators intended.

Union or Confederate, the memorials speak of memories held sacred.

1.
EAST TEXAS MONUMENTS

Huntsville, Walker County

HUNTSVILLE IS AT THE JUNCTION of Interstate 45, U.S. Highway 190, and state highways 19 and 30. The monument is downtown on the courthouse lawn, at the corner of Eleventh Street (U.S. Highway 190) and Sam Houston Avenue.

Responding to veteran J. F. Jarrard's call, twenty-five local women gathered at the Baptist church on a Sunday afternoon in November 1899 to establish a UDC chapter in Huntsville, which they named the John B. Gordon Chapter after Gen. John B. Gordon, a respected soldier and, later, a governor and senator from Georgia. In 1900 the chapter's second president, Mary Wynne Farris, suggested erecting a monument to the Confederacy. Farris, born in Mississippi in 1836, came to Texas as a child with her parents and was in the first graduating class of Andrew Female College, one of the earliest schools for girls in the state. The petite, dark-haired woman worked until her death in 1922 to raise funds to commemorate the county's soldiers. On June 27, 1956, more than fifty years after Farris first began raising money, the Gordon Chapter erected a small marble shaft on the courthouse lawn "in memory of our Confederate patriots." The monument was removed and placed in storage in 1968 after the courthouse burned, but was placed on the grounds of the new courthouse in June 1973.[1]

Jefferson, Marion County

Jefferson is at the intersection of U.S. Highway 59 and State High-

Huntsville monument. Author photograph.

way 49. The monument sits on the courthouse lawn on West Austin Street.

Jefferson's Richard Taylor Camp, UCV, unveiled its Confederate monument on July 10, 1907, six blocks north of its present location on the courthouse lawn. Although members of the camp and nearby Robert E. Lee Chapter of the UDC had debated the merits of erecting a monument for several years, the two organizations garnered little public support until the neighboring city of Marshall unveiled a memorial in January 1906. So many Jeffersonians participated in the ceremonies in Marshall that Jefferson's citizens vowed to build their own monument to the Confederacy, a memorial that would, of course, surpass Marshall's.[2]

The Richard Taylor Camp—called the Dick Taylor Camp by the old soldiers and named in honor of Gen. Richard Taylor, hero of the Battle of Mansfield, Louisiana, and son of President Zachary Taylor—placed an order with Llano, Texas, granite dealer Frank Teich for a shaft of granite topped by a Confederate soldier of gray bronze. The camp originally planned to place the monument in Oakwood Cemetery but decided instead, after the memorial's arrival, to set it in a small park (only 115 by 150 feet) on the north side of Broadway at the corner of Line and Polk Street, six blocks north of the courthouse and town square.[3]

Jefferson's city leaders organized an unveiling celebration that included a parade, cannon fire, and a musical program, all with an eye to outdoing Marshall's recent ceremony. United States Senator Charles Allen Culberson, who had spent his childhood in Jefferson (Culberson was six years old when the war began) and had been elected in 1894 and 1896 as the state's governor, served as the primary speaker at the celebration. The large crowd that gathered sang "Tenting on the Old Camp Ground" and then listened to a dedicatory address delivered by Gertrude Cartwright of the Robert E. Lee Chapter of the UDC in Cass County. Jefferson's newspaper, the *Jimplecute*, said her speech "stirred the heart of every Southerner." Although the veterans spearheaded the monument drive, they committed the monument's care to the Robert E. Lee Chapter, telling the members that the monument was "a gift to be cherished and protected."[4]

At the end of the ceremony, the crowd sang the "Bonnie Blue Flag" while thirteen girls dressed in white dresses with red sashes, each one representing one of the Confederate states, placed wreaths of flowers at the monument's base and then pulled ribbons that released the red, white, and blue bunting draped over the monument. As soon as the bronze Confederate figure came into view, the crowd let out a prolonged cheer, mingled with the rebel yell. Senator Culberson claimed, "no community in the state responded to the call to arms of 1861 with more honor, sympathy, or daring soldiery than Jefferson."[5]

In the 1930s Joseph McCasland became county judge and had the monument moved from its original location to the courthouse. Since boyhood, McCasland had argued with his father that the monument should be moved, and he was especially appalled that it stood with its back facing the North. After becoming county judge, he "had the county surveyor determine true North, and then I had the Confederate monument relocated on the courthouse lawn so that the soldier's eyes would be gazing right toward his enemy."[6]

For seventy-five years, local history buffs attempted to solve the mystery of the monument's lost inscription. Like many monuments in Texas, Jefferson's provided the name of the UCV camp that erected the statue plus a few other lines, in this case, "lest we forget. In memory of our dead. 1861–1865." But unlike other memorials, Jefferson's monument had a line erased from the monument. By the mid-1980s a myth circulated that the words "for a lost cause," had been inscribed on the monument but were rubbed off in 1911 when survivors of Hood's Brigade met in Jefferson for a reunion. According to the myth, the old soldiers noticed the inscription, declared, "Hell, it was no Lost Cause," and removed the offensive statement.[7]

Curious researchers tried many different methods for deciphering the missing lines. Eventually one man tried liberally dusting the scrawled inscription with ladies' face powder and a powder puff. It soon became clear that the last word began with a "C" and possibly ended with a "Y." Soon, the letter "W" became evident, as did the letters "OO" in the second word. Jotting down the letters, the researcher speculated about the missing ones. Suddenly the inscription was obvious—"In Oakwood Cemetery." Newspaper accounts in early 1907 regarding the monument selection recounted that the Dick Taylor Camp had been uncertain whether to place the monument in the park, or in the cemetery, where so many Confederate dead were buried. Apparently the monument had been ordered with the idea that it would be placed in the cemetery but by the time it arrived, the camp had decided to place it in the park.[8]

Linden, Cass County

Linden is at the intersection of U.S. Highway 59 and state highways 8 and 155. The monument is on the courthouse lawn on East Houston Street.

Gertrude Curtwright missed her younger brother terribly after the war. He died while serving the Confederate cause, and no matter how many years passed, Curtwright could not forget her only brother. In 1903 she convinced area veterans and businessmen that the county needed a monument to honor her brother and all the men like him who had given their lives fighting for a free and independent South. Local citizens agreed and collected $320 to purchase their monument—a marble shaft which they placed in the "most public of places," the lawn of the county courthouse. They unveiled the monument in October 1903.[9]

The *Cass County Sun* reported that the unveiling ceremony began at ten o'clock in the morning with the Atlanta Band leading the procession (the musicians hailed from the nearby town of Atlanta, not the city in Georgia). Gertrude Curtwright spoke, the newspaper reporter claiming that "she made one of the best speeches that it has been our pleasure to listen to for a while." Curtwright spoke frequently in front of large crowds. Her granddaughter later recalled that she once delivered an address to a large group of veterans gathered for a reunion in New Orleans, and when she finished, the veterans cheered her words loudly. Curtwright seemed at ease in the spotlight. Not only was she the only woman to speak that day, but she was also the only female member of the monument committee; that might not seem unusual considering that Curtwright had been the one to suggest building the memorial, but it was highly unusual for women to serve on decision-making committees. Women often suggested that a monument should be built, and they almost always did the necessary fundraising, but men generally kept the planning committees to themselves. Local men seemed comfortable with women doing the bulk of the work, but few relinquished the decision-making roles.[10]

Cass County's courthouse is the oldest continually used courthouse in the state. Area builders began constructing the structure in 1859 but did not finish the courthouse until 1866, their work having been interrupted by the war. Although a fire gutted the courthouse in 1933, the county restored its interior, repaired the damage to the exterior, and reopened the following year. But this fire was not the courthouse's only brush with danger.[11]

A tornado blew through Linden on May 13, 1908, destroying much of the town and leaving hundreds homeless. The Confederate monument blew over in the storm, and the city hired Nelson & Sheffield (more than likely a local granite dealer) to replace it the following November. A strong wind once again toppled the memorial in September 1940, and the community hired the T. J. Hopkins Studio of Atlanta, Texas, to shorten the monument and place it back on its base. This appears to have worked: the shortened monument, dedicated "in memory of our Confederate soldiers who fought and died in the war and of those who fought and lived," stands on the courthouse lawn today.[12]

Livingston, Polk County

Livingston is at the junction of U.S. highways 190 and 59 and State Highway 146. The monument sits on the courthouse lawn on Church Street.

The Ike Turner Camp, UCV, erected the Confederate monument in Livingston on October 10, 1900. The single granite shaft has inscriptions on all four sides, including one that states, "Polk County furnished the Confederacy more soldiers than she had voters."[13]

Polk County boasts that nine hundred of its area men joined the Confederacy between 1861 and 1865, forming seven separate companies, while it had only six hundred registered voters in 1860. The county also claims that it provided a greater number of slaves and servants for the cause, in proportion to its white population, than did any other Texas county.[14]

In 1996 an architect working for the city suggested that the monument be moved from the courthouse lawn to another location and that a gazebo be built in its place. A few citizens rallied to stop the move, and the memorial still stands where it was originally unveiled in 1900.[15]

Longview, Gregg County

Longview is at Interstate 20 and U.S. highways 80 and 259. The monument is on the courthouse lawn on East Methvin Street.

"God bless the noble women who have made this great day possible," declared Longview's Mayor G. A. Bodenheim in his speech at the city's monument unveiling ceremony. After six years of fundraising, the R. B. Levy Chapter of the UDC erected a monument of Texas granite and Italian marble on June 3, 1911, in commemoration of Jefferson Davis's birth.[16]

The city organized a massive celebration. Led by a local band, citizens marched to the monument waving flags and bunting of red and white. Crowding around the memorial, the audience listened as Mayor Bodenheim and Viola Bivins, president of the Levy Chapter, spoke of their love for the men who fought for the Confederacy. Bivins declared that the old soldiers would "live eternally in the hearts and ideals of their children." Her speech, the longest of the ceremony, marked one of the first times in Longview that a woman had been asked to speak to such a large mixed-sex gathering.[17]

The monument was unveiled with great ceremony, and when the public first saw the statue, waves of cheers, which some citizens said were reminiscent of the old rebel yell, went through the crowd. Longview's Chamber of Commerce invited everyone to the courthouse lawn where they and the Levy Chapter of the UDC had organized a barbeque dinner. Following the meal, the city's citizens continued the celebration with a baseball game, a motorcycle race, and a release of balloons.[18]

Originally placed within sight of the train depot so that all visitors would immediately see the memorial, the monument was unveiled in Bodie Park, which the city created specifically for the monument. For years the park served as a meeting place for local citizens. In 1930, after the discovery of oil in East Texas, the city sold the park for commercial development, and the memorial was moved to the courthouse lawn, where it still stands.[19]

The thirty-five-foot monument was designed by Llano granite dealer Frank Teich at an estimated cost of $3,000. A life-size figure of a Confederate soldier stands above a marble base decorated with a statue of a woman writing the words "Lest We Forget" on a tablet.[20]

Marshall, Harrison County

Marshall is on Interstate 20, approximately thirty-nine miles west of Shreveport, Louisiana. The city's main Confederate monument sits on the old courthouse lawn on Whetstone Square (in the old downtown district). There is a second monument in the northwest corner of the city cemetery on Lynoak Street.

Laura Elgin, president of Marshall Chapter of the UDC, almost single-handedly ensured the creation of the town's main memorial. Calling the work a "labor of love," Elgin began fundraising in 1903. Three years later on January 19, 1906 (in commemoration of Robert E. Lee's birth), she and the Marshall Chapter unveiled the sculpture on the courthouse lawn, in the same spot where several Confederate companies—the most notable being Bass's Grays, also known as Company D, Seventh Texas Regiment, commanded by K. M. Van Zandt—had been sworn into service.[21]

The Marshall Chapter of the UDC purchased the most prominent memorial from Llano granite dealer Frank Teich for an estimated $2,500. The sculpture stands nineteen feet tall and is topped by a soldier figure with a blanket rolled around his shoulder alongside a haversack and canteen. A Confederate flag, entwined with a laurel wreath and palm leaf, decorates the east side of the base. The wreath was chosen to represent the charge and the palm leaf the grief for those who lost their lives following the Confederate flag.[22] The Daughters inscribed the memorial's north and south sides with poems that lament the dead:

> Take our love and our tears today; take them, all that we have to give,
> And by God's help while our heart shall live it still shall keep in its
> Thankful way the campfires lit for the men in gray—
> "Aye till trumpet sounds far away and the silver bugles of heaven play,
> And the roll is called at the judgment day![23]

The unveiling ceremony began at ten o'clock in the morning with a parade of veterans and UDC members leading Marshall's citizens to

Dr. Blocker, A. G. Adams. Wm Heartsill - Mrs. Elgin.
Tom Elgin - E. J. Fry - Tom Whaley.
Statue unveiled Jan. 1906.

Marshall's moment with key individuals associated with the monument erection, including Laura Elgin, president of the Marshall Chapter of the UDC. Photograph courtesy of the Harrison County Historical Museum, Marshall, Tex.

the courthouse. Thirteen young girls, representing the thirteen states of the Confederacy, formed a ring around the monument and sang "My Maryland." A band played other songs, including "America" and the "Vacant Chair," and a loud cheer went through the audience when the musicians played "Dixie." The main speakers of the day were Laura Elgin, Dr. A. G. Clopton, a veteran, and W. W. Heartsill, who later wrote a book recording his wartime experiences.[24]

K. M. Van Zandt, who had organized one of the first companies from Marshall to enlist in the Confederacy, returned to the city for the unveiling ceremony and recounted how at that exact spot in 1861 his mustered company was presented with a flag made by the women of the city. When it came time to surrender, he said, the men tore the flag into little bits, each member taking a tiny souvenir, rather than surrendering their banner.[25]

A second, much smaller monument sits in Marshall's city cemetery. The Marshall Chapter of the UDC erected the granite shaft in 1908 to honor the unknown Confederate soldiers buried in the cemetery.[26]

Mount Pleasant, Titus County

Mount Pleasant is sixty-one miles southwest of Texarkana at the junction of Interstate 30, U.S. Highway 271, and State Highway 49. The monument is on the courthouse square on West First Street.

The Dudley W. Jones Camp, UCV, sponsored several reunions in Mount Pleasant around the turn of the twentieth century. The veterans named their camp in honor of Dudley Jones, the son of one of the county's earliest pioneers, who rushed back to Texas from his law studies in Tennessee at the first sign of secession and enlisted in the Ninth Texas Cavalry. He eventually rose to

Mt. Pleasant's monument was likely ordered from one of the many monument companies operating in the South at the turn of the twentieth century. Author photograph.

the rank of colonel and commanding officer of the company. Jones survived the war but died in Houston in 1870. His fellow soldiers honored his memory by naming their camp for him.[27]

Very little is known about Mount Pleasant's Confederate monument. The Jones UCV Camp, in conjunction with the county UDC organization, erected the monument, most likely in 1911, although fundraising began several years before the unveiling. The Daughters collected most of the funds by asking for subscriptions and selling sandwiches and pies downtown on Saturdays and other days when crowds gathered in town for business or pleasure.[28]

The granite monument is topped by a statue of a Confederate soldier at parade rest and an unfurled flag is inscribed on the pillar. The figure of the soldier was probably ordered from one of the many monument catalogs available at the time because an identical monument was built in Mississippi in 1908. The city improved upon the monument's placement by creating a concrete base to keep the wagons that gathered around the square from getting too close to the monument and possibly damaging it.[29]

Palestine, Anderson County

Palestine is at the intersection of U.S. highways 79 and 287. The John H. Reagan Memorial is in Reagan Park at the corner of Reagan Street and Crockett Road.

The John H. Reagan Chapter of the UDC worked for many years to raise the necessary funds to build a statue to honor their most famous citizen, John H. Reagan, who served as postmaster general and secretary of the treasury of the Confederate States of America. After the war Reagan won a seat in the U.S. House of Representatives and then in the Senate, and before his death he served as chairman of the Railroad Commission of Texas.[30]

Despite their efforts, the Daughters had difficulty raising money for a monument until after Reagan's death in 1905 when they advertised in the *Confederate Veteran* magazine, asking all Southerners who had admired Reagan in life to honor him by contributing to the monument. Having secured partial funding, the UDC chapter held a competition for the design of the monument and unanimously chose that of Italian sculptor and San Antonio resident Pompeo Coppini.[31]

The memorial consists of two larger-than-life figures, cast in bronze at the Nelli Foundry in Rome, Italy. Standing upon a nine-foot-high base of Texas granite, the figure of Reagan is depicted as having just risen from his seat in the senate with his hand extended in a gesture of command. At his feet sits the allegorical representation of a defeated Roman soldier called *The Lost Cause*. The figure is portrayed in contemplation with a Confederate flag draped across his lap and thirteen stars, representing the thirteen Confederate states, mounted on the front of his helmet.[32]

The Daughters originally planned to place the monument at the heart of the city on Spring Street where it was intersected by Magnolia and Palmer streets. Only the monument's base was built on this spot because shortly afterward the city purchased the land that now forms Reagan Park and decided to place the monument in the park and name the green space for Reagan. The memorial was unveiled on July 6, 1911, where it presently stands, but few citizens attended the small ceremony. The monument plus the amount it cost to move the base and pave the area where the pedestal sits cost an estimated $2,950.[33]

Extensive vandalism forced the city to restore the monument in 1967. The Dogwood Garden Club has since maintained it and the surrounding grounds.[34]

Rusk, Cherokee County

Rusk is at the junction of U.S. highways 69 and 84 and State Highway 110. The monument sits on the courthouse lawn on the corner of North Main and Henderson streets.

Cherokee County veterans began the drive to erect a monument to the county's Confederate dead in 1899 but could not raise adequate funds until the city's Frank Taylor Chapter of the UDC took over the fundraising. The UDC succeeded where the veterans had failed, and the city's monument was unveiled on the site of the county's third courthouse on October 3, 1907.[35]

A life-size statue of a soldier stands atop the memorial, and the granite base is inscribed on all four sides, two of which include poems celebrating the Confederate soldier:

> Their own true hearts and dauntless arms have covered them with glory.

And while a southerner treads the soil they live in song and glory.

Some beneath the sod of distant states their patient hearts have laid, where, with strangers' heedless haste their unwatched graves were made.[36]

The city moved the memorial to the lawn of the present courthouse when it was built in 1921, and the site became a gathering place for countywide celebrations. One of the largest of these assemblies occurred on November 11, 1921, when the county's living Confederate veterans gathered to honor the community's World War I veterans. The county is currently attempting to raise funds to restore the monument.[37]

Scottsville, Harrison County

Scottsville is on farm-to-market roads (FM) 1998 and 2199, four miles east of Marshall. The monument is at the entrance of Scottsville's city cemetery on FM 1998, east of the city just past the intersection of FM 2199.

Leading citizen and president of Scottsville's Commercial Nation Bank, Capt. Peter Youree, and his wife, Elizabeth Scott Youree, donated the eighteen-foot marble statue of a young Confederate private in 1915 in memory of the city's Confederate soldiers. It stands guard over the 145-year-old cemetery.[38]

The Scottville Cemetery has the largest collection of Llano granite dealer Frank Teich's memorials in the state, as well as several beautiful molds ordered from Italy through catalogs. The Youree family erected another prominent monument, *Weeping Angel*, which they placed in the cemetery in memory of their only son, William Scott Youree, who died in childhood. Behind it stands a stone chapel with hand-hewn cypress pews and stained-glass windows, also a monument to William Youree.[39]

Vandals ravaged the Scottsville Cemetery in 1987, and although repairs were made, many of the monuments were not restored to their former beauty.[40]

Texarkana, Bowie County

Texarkana is at the junction of Interstate 30 and U.S. highways 59, 67, 71, and 82 on the Texas-Arkansas border. The monument is at

United Daughters of the Confederacy Park on Fifth Street and State Line Avenue.

Veteran James Thomas Rosborough funded Texarkana's *Soldiers and Mothers of the Confederacy* memorial, the only monument in the state dedicated to the women of the South. Rosborough purchased the land on which the monument sits from the Episcopal Diocese and deeded it to the cities of Texarkana (in Texas and Arkansas) and the UDC. The site was chosen because of its central location.[41]

Rosborough ordered the larger-than-life-size memorial from the Albert Weiblem Marble and Granite Company in New Orleans for $10,000 on February 28, 1917. Carved in Leghorn, Italy, the monument failed to arrive in Texarkana until the spring of 1918 because World War I disrupted the shipment of goods overseas. The subsequent unveiling ceremony on April 21, 1918 was particularly moving for many citizens who were caught up in a heightened sense of patriotism because of the world war.[42]

The monument features the statue of a Confederate private above a square formed by four marble pillars on which a female figure sits, representing the mothers of Southern soldiers. The following inscription is carved into the memorial:

O Great Confederate Mothers, we would print your names on monuments, that men may read them as the years go and tribute pay to you who boreand nurtured hero-sons and gave them solace on that darkest hour, whenthey came home with broken swords and guns.[43]

Tyler, Smith County

Tyler is ninety-nine miles southeast of Dallas at the junction of U.S. highways 69 and 271 and state highways 14, 31, 64, 110, and 155. The monument is in Oakwood Cemetery on the 700 block of Oakwood Street.

The Mollie Moore Davis Chapter of the UDC kicked off the city's monument fundraising drive with an "Old Fiddlers Contest." The ladies invited all old-time fiddlers to participate in the event at the Grand Opera House, which they decorated with flowers, greenery (magnolias, cape jasmine, roses, evergreens, and lilies), and Confederate battle flags. One Daughter said of the concert, which netted $400, "It was fine, and the people enjoyed it ever so much. It set one's heart busy with memory, and the good old days rose from the dust of recollection and trooped before the mind's eye, and the mists that obscure the long ago cleared away and formed a pretty halo around the past."[44]

With fundraising well under way, the UDC chapter purchased a statue from Morris Brothers Marble Works in Tyler, which made the marble base locally and ordered the figure of a soldier from Italy. The base was set in 1907, but when they uncrated the statue, Morris Brothers discovered a large crack on the face of the soldier. The figure was returned to Italy for repair, delaying the unveiling for two years.[45]

The unveiling ceremony finally took place on July 10, 1909. Starting at the post office, the city's citizens paraded to Oakwood Cemetery. Following speeches and music, a crowd estimated at 8,000 people enjoyed a public dinner on the courthouse square.[46]

2.
NORTH TEXAS MONUMENTS

Bonham, Fannin County

BONHAM IS AT THE JUNCTION of U.S. Highway 82 and state highways 78 and 121, twelve miles south of the Red River. The monument sits on the courthouse lawn on West Sam Rayburn Drive.

Bonham's newspaper, the *Fannin County Favorite*, encouraged local citizens in July 1905 to "take a few days off, wash up the children, get your wife a new dress, fill your baskets full and then hitch up old Jack and Beek and come down to the county seat for a few days of jollification" at the county's combined Old Settler's Day and United Confederate Veterans Reunion. Despite a rain delay of one week, Bonham's residents needed little encouragement and most came out to enjoy the festivities and renew old acquaintances.[1]

A highlight of the event was the unveiling of the county's Confederate monument. The local UDC chapter, along with the Confederate Veterans Association of Fannin County, hired Bonham Marble Works to erect a memorial at a cost of $2,500, paid for by public subscription.[2]

The granite statue, carved in Italy, stands twenty-eight-feet high and was modeled after a painting of a young Tennessee soldier named Samuel Davis who was captured and hanged as a spy in Tennessee. For Southerners after the war, the name "Sam Davis" came to represent the justness of their cause and the bravery of the people themselves. Davis died at age nineteen because he refused to name the Northern traitor who had given him vital war information. Davis emerged after his death as a cultural icon of the Lost Cause movement. In addition to being the model for Bonham's monument, Davis's image is represented in several other memorials across the region.[3]

Clarksville, Red River County

Clarksville is at the junction of U.S. Highway 82, State Highway 37, and farm-to-market roads 114, 412, 909, 910, and 1159. The monument is on the city square on the 100 block of Broadway.

The Clarksville Chapter of the UDC gave the citizens of Red River County a granite statue of a Confederate soldier at parade rest in honor of the John C. Burks Camp, UCV. The monument, erected in the 1920s, faced northeast and greeted visitors as they arrived in town from the train station.[4]

The Clarksville John C. Burks Camp was organized in the summer of 1890 and remained active until the last veteran died in June 1942. With 127 charter members, the camp eventually swelled to over 600 members. The camp held its annual reunion on the more than twenty acres owned by the veterans a half-mile northeast of town. For more than thirty years, the reunion of former soldiers was a social highlight and thousands of Texans attended, enjoying music, speeches, fine food, entertainment, and an opportunity to reminisce and socialize.[5]

Denison, Grayson County

Denison is on U.S. highways 75 and 69, seven miles north of Sherman. The monument is in the Fairview Cemetery on U.S. Highway 75-A, north of town.

The monument in Denison's Fairview Cemetery is one of only three in Texas that celebrates the Union. The life-size granite figure of a U.S. soldier was erected in 1906 by the Nathaniel Lyon Post 5, Grand Army of the Republic, Department of Texas organization and its auxiliary, the Woman's Relief Corp, Chapter 2.[6]

Memorializing the remains of six Union soldiers who settled in Grayson County after the war, the monument was designed locally by A. P. Chamberlain, owner of Denison Marble Works. Most likely, Chamberlain carved the base but ordered the figure from a granite dealer's mail-order catalog.[7]

Denison attracted quite a few Northerners after the war. The

Union monument in Denison at Fairview Cemetery. Photograph courtesy of Mike Price from http://www.texasescapes.com/Monuments/Denison-Texas-Union-Soldier-Statue-and-Memorial.htm.

county, with very few cultural ties to the Deep South, had voted against secession in 1861 by a vote of 901 to 463.[8]

Denton, Denton County

Denton is on Interstate 35, where it forks to become 35E to Dallas and 35W to Fort Worth. The monument is on the south entrance of the courthouse lawn on West Hickory Street.

The Katie Daffan Chapter of the UDC was formed in Denton in 1905 with ten charter members. Named in honor of one of Texas's most prominent clubwomen and president of the Texas UDC at the time, the group immediately began to raise money for a monument, which was erected on June 3, 1918. The granite memorial consists of a large arch surmounted by a figure of marble representing a young Confederate soldier. The two columns supporting the arch are equipped with twin drinking fountains.[9]

The monument became the focus of controversy in June 1999 when the county's historical commission sought funding to repair the drinking fountains. An African American community activist protested efforts to repair the monument and demanded that it be removed from its central location. A week later, he changed his position and offered to head a committee to restore the memorial and attach a plaque noting that blacks were once barred from drinking from the "whites only" fountain. Such controversy has surrounded many of Texas's Confederate monuments. Civil rights activists claim that memorials to the Confederacy glorify an army that fought to perpetuate slavery.[10]

Denton's Confederate monument still stands at the entrance of the courthouse lawn—the water fountains have not been repaired.

Gainesville, Cooke County

Gainesville is on Interstate 35, sixty-seven miles north of Dallas. The city has two Confederate monuments, one on the courthouse lawn on Main and Commerce Streets and the other near the entrance of Leonard Park off California Street.

The Lou Doughtery Chapter of the UDC dedicated Gainesville's primary Confederate monument, located downtown on the courthouse lawn, on June 3, 1908, to the "heroes of the South." While the monument celebrated the Confederate soldier, the Daughters' unveiling cer-

Close-up of Confederate soldier on top of monument in Denton. Author photograph.

emony emphasized the women of the 1860s who "by sacrifice and management made possible the maintenance of an army to defend country and rights." The featured speaker at the memorial's unveiling, Mrs. J. M. Wright, president of the Lou Doughtery Chapter, spoke not only about the "sacrifice and management" of the Southern women but of their ability to inspire future generations. The monument's presence, Wright asserted, would perpetuate the principles for which the mothers of the South had lived, fought, and died.[11]

The monument's inscription reflects the Daughters' desire to celebrate their mothers:

> To the women of the Confederacy, whose pious ministrations
> to our wounded soldiers and sailors soothed the last hours of
> those who died far from the objects of their tenderest love; and

whose patriotism will teach their children to emulate the deeds of their revolutionary sires."

The Lou Doughtery Chapter erected Gainesville's other Confederate monument, in Leonard Park, on February 15, 1908. This monument is dedicated simply to "our heroes." Both monuments are granite shafts topped by life-size figures of young Confederate soldiers. There is an additional Civil War marker in Gainesville of historical significance. Moved downtown to the banks of Pecan Creek in 1999, the marker commemorates the location of the Great Hanging at Gainesville in 1862, when local citizens, fearful of a Northern invasion and a local peace party of Union sympathizers, arrested local men accused of being loyal to the federal government. Texas Confederates convened a citizens court, tried the men for treason, hanged forty of them, and shot two who were attempting to escape.[12]

Paris, Lamar County
Paris is at the junction of U.S. highways 271 and 82. The monument sits on the lawn of the county courthouse on Lamar (U.S. 82) and North Main (U.S. 271) streets.

The Lamar Chapter of the UDC selected and purchased plans to build a Confederate monument in early 1902. The chapter then sent the blueprints to several sculptors for bids. When Pompeo Coppini, an Italian-born sculptor who had immigrated to San Antonio, received a copy, he decried the "monstrous design," immediately boarded a train for Paris, and met with the monument committee before bidding for the commission.[13]

Coppini later wrote in his autobiography, "I begged them never to go through with the erection of another disgrace to the noble Southern cause. . . . I saw in it [the monument's design] a possible chance to convince that committee that they were about to commit a crime, which, while unintentional, would cause a permanent injury to the advancement in art in the South."[14]

Coppini had not brought materials with him, but the committee seemed so interested in his arguments that he went to a local store where schoolbooks and stationery were sold and bought a few sheets of children's drawing paper, a small ruler, and a pencil. He spent the

Coppini's monument in Paris, which he claimed began his sculpting career in the state. Author photograph.

night in his hotel room creating a scale drawing of a figure of a Confederate soldier on top of a pedestal and four busts adorning the base, representing Gen. Robert E. Lee, Jefferson Davis, Albert Sidney Johnston, and Gen. Thomas "Stonewall" Jackson. The next day Coppini received the commission and signed a contract to sculpt the monument for $4,600. According to the artist, this commission marked the beginning of his career as a sculptor in Texas.[15]

The monument of granite and bronze was designed and sculpted by Coppini, and Otto Zirkel of San Antonio built the stone portions. The Lamar Chapter of the UDC collected donations and subscriptions of over $5,000 to defray the costs of the monument. The largest benefactor was the chapter's president, Mary America Aikin Connor, who also donated large amounts of money to other causes in Paris, including the Aikin Hospital and the Mary Connor College for Girls.[16]

Sherman, Grayson County

Sherman is seventy-five miles north of Dallas on U.S. Highway 75. The monument sits on the courthouse lawn on the corner of Houston (State Highway 56) and Lamar streets.

The city of Sherman claims that its monument, unveiled on April 21, 1897, was the first memorial erected to the Confederacy in Texas. In fact, a memorial had been placed earlier in Waco (1893), but Sherman's was the first to include a statue of a Confederate soldier and one of only three bronze figures erected prior to the turn of the century, the other two being on the grounds of the capital in Austin.[17]

Originally, the Mildred Lee Camp, UCV, and the Dixie Chapter of the UDC planned to erect a memorial shaft in the city cemetery, but the fundraising committee believed that given time, the county's citizens would contribute enough funds to build a larger monument to place downtown on the courthouse lawn.[18]

After six years of sponsoring subscriptions, concerts, dinners, lawn parties, ice cream festivals, as well as soliciting private donations, the veterans and Daughters had collected more than $5,000 to purchase a monument from E. T. Bergen and Company of Fort Worth. The monument consists of three sections: a twelve-foot-square base of blue-gray granite quarried at Stone Mountain, Georgia; a ten-foot pedestal that tapers toward the top; and a larger-than-life-size bronze figure of a Confederate soldier standing at attention. From base to top, the monument stands forty-three-feet tall.[19]

A newspaper reporter described the day-long unveiling ceremony, saying that "every window was filled with people. The sidewalks were so jammed that passage through them could not be effected, and the streets were literally packed with a surging mass of humanity." More than twenty thousand people gathered for the unveiling ceremony, which featured a parade consisting of two bands, a fife and drum corps, five UCV camps, students from five colleges, one thousand schoolchildren carrying wreaths, and members of the Odd Fellows and Woodsmen of the World. After the Daughters unveiled the monument, men in the crowd fired their guns and cried out the Rebel yell. Women placed garlands around the base of the monument, and loyal Southerners sang "In the Sweet Bye and Bye." Ironically, Grayson County had voted almost two to one against secession in 1861.[20]

3.
NORTH CENTRAL TEXAS MONUMENTS

Cleburne, Johnson County

CLEBURNE IS ON U.S. HIGHWAY 67, thirty miles south of Fort Worth. The town's primary monument sits on the courthouse lawn at the intersection of Main (State Highway 174) and Henderson (U.S. Highway 67) streets. There is a memorial arch in Cleburne Memorial Cemetery dedicated to the Confederacy. The cemetery is on East Washington Street off U.S. Highway 67.

The Pat Cleburne Chapter of the UDC erected the city's main monument downtown on December 6, 1917. The memorial consists of a shaft atop a large public drinking basin. The entire height of the memorial is over twenty-eight feet. The sixty-eight members of the Pat Cleburne Camp raised $2,750 to erect the monument.[1]

The monumental arch in Confederate Memorial Park Cemetery, Cleburne. Author photograph.

These veterans also erected the arch that stands in the southwest corner of Cleburne's Memorial Cemetery. Dedicated in 1921, the concrete arch served as the front gate to the cemetery

44

and symbolically joined it with Confederate Memorial Park, an area of land owned by the veterans. The old soldiers met for their yearly reunion in the park until the Cleburne Camp disbanded (because so few veterans were left). At that time the park became part of the cemetery, which contains the graves of many Confederate veterans.[2]

Corsicana, Navarro County

Corsicana is fifty-eight miles southeast of Dallas at the junction of Interstate 45 and U.S. highways 75 and 287. The monument sits on the courthouse lawn at the corner of West Third Street and Thirteenth Avenue.

The Navarro Chapter of the UDC was formed in 1897, primarily to erect a monument to the Confederacy. By 1907 the chapter had raised enough money to acquire a nine-foot figure, cast in bronze, of a soldier with a raised bugle. Designed by Italian sculptor Louis Amateis, the monument was named *Call to Arms*. The Daughters purchased it from the Bureau Brothers Bronze Founders in Philadelphia.[3]

More than a thousand local citizens attended the monument's unveiling on January 20, 1908. Among shouts and cheers, thirteen girls, each holding a small Confederate flag, pulled cords on a cloth to uncover the monument. Afterward the girls led the crowd in singing "Bonnie Blue Flag." The city's newspaper summarized the ceremony activities, relating that they included a speech by Judge R. E. Prince, who paid tribute to the "valor of southern soldiers and southern women" and the reading of a poem, "The Tear Stained Banner," by Mrs. M. D. Peck, president of the local UDC chapter.[4]

The statue of the Confederate bugler calling his comrades to arms rests on a ten-foot pedestal of marble. Inscriptions surround all four sides and include this lament, first published in the *Confederate Veteran* in January 1904:

> Tell it as you may
> It never can be told
> Sing it as you will
> It never can be sung
> The story of the glory
> Of the men who wore the gray

Dallas, Dallas County

Dallas is at the crossroads of interstates 20, 30, 35, and 45. There are several monuments in the city. The primary memorial is on the grounds of the city's convention center, which is next to the Masonic and Pioneer Cemeteries off Young Street. Monuments are also located in Lee Park at the corner of Hall Street and Turtle Creek Boulevard, in Fair Park on the Centennial Building, and in Greenwood Cemetery at 3020 Oak Grove Street.

Katie Cabell Currie Muse, founder and first president of the Texas Division of the United Daughters of the Confederacy. Photograph courtesy of the Dallas Historical Society.

The Dallas Chapter of the UDC erected the first public monument in the city on April 29, 1897. Led by Katie Cabell Currie Muse, founder of the organization's Texas division, the chapter raised more than $5,000 and hired Frank Teich of Llano, Texas, to design the memorial. The monument stands sixty-feet tall and consists of a central shaft topped by a Confederate soldier at rest, reportedly modeled after local businessman W. H. Gaston. Four lesser columns surround the center, each bearing a single nine-foot sculpture of one of four prominent Confederates: Jefferson Davis, Robert E. Lee, "Stonewall" Thomas Jackson, and Albert Sidney Johnston.[5]

The Daughters unveiled the large monument in City Park during a weekend-long flurry of activities, which included a fancy-dress ball, a large feast in honor of the veterans, and (according to the *Dallas Morning News*) the longest, "most imposing" parade in Dallas's history. The newspaper estimated that more than 42,000 Texans attended the unveiling ceremony.[6]

Equally exciting for many of the city's residents was the Dallas Southern Memorial Association's unveiling of the *Robert E. Lee on Traveler* memorial. Canadian sculptor Alexander Phimister Proctor completed the double-equestrian bronze statue in 1935, and President

Dallas's Confederate Monument prior to being moved to the grounds of the Convention Center. Photograph courtesy of the Dallas Historical Society.

Franklin D. Roosevelt attended its unveiling ceremony on June 12, 1936, declaring the memorial "magnificent."[7]

Proctor studied photographs of Lee and his horse before creating a working model—a project that lasted more than four years. An aide riding next to Lee represents "the entire youth of the South to whom Lee became a great inspiration." The monument cost $50,000, which the Dallas Southern Monument Association raised over a period of eight years; they also erected a small fountain across the street from the Lee monument in Turtle Creek Lake as a tribute to all Confederate heroes.[8]

In 1936, as part of the construction of the Centennial Building in Fair Park, the Texas Centennial Exposition Corporation hired Laurence Tenney Stevens to sculpt a series of allegorical female figures representing the six flags under which Texas had been ruled. *The Confederate*, a figure fashioned out of concrete, forms part of a three-figure grouping on a base. This figure wears a band of seven stars around her head, to represent the fact that Texas was the seventh state to secede from the Union and join the Confederacy.[9]

In 1901 the Dallas Chapter of the UDC erected a small statue of a Confederate soldier in Greenwood Cemetery. The seven-foot marble memorial marks the grave of Captain S. P. Emerson, a wealthy Dallas businessman who moved to Texas from Kentucky after the war. During the war, Emerson fought at Fort Donelson in northern Tennessee. When the fort fell to Ulysses S. Grant in 1862, the Confederate soldier refused to surrender, escaping instead by swimming and wading across the Cumberland River, which butted against the fort. The memorial cost $5,000, provided for by Emerson's will, and honors both Emerson and the thirty-six Confederate soldiers buried beside him. All of the men's graves face south.[10]

Ennis, Ellis County

Ennis is at the intersection of Interstate 45 and state highways 34, 75, and 287. The monument is in Myrtle Cemetery in the older section, Tract 1, off Glasscock Road (accessible from West Ennis Avenue).

On April 29, 1906 the Daffan-Latimer Chapter of the UDC erected a granite obelisk in Myrtle Cemetery to the "memory of Confederate soldiers." The monument is inscribed with the

Katie Daffan, twice president of the Texas Division of the United Daughters of the Confederacy and president of the national UDC. Photograph courtesy of the Austin History Center, Austin Public Library.

phrases, "the truth will live" and "in memory of the brave men who gave all to their country by the children of the Confederacy." [11]

The Daughters named their chapter after one of the town's most famous women, Katie Daffan, a longtime Ennis resident who gained statewide fame as a newspaper journalist, novelist, poet, and storyteller. Daffan served on several state boards, including the state's public textbook selection committee, and worked for many years as the supervisor of the Texas Confederate Woman's Home. Unmarried—she had a brief marriage that ended in divorce—Daffan earned a living by writing and teaching school. She devoted her free time to women's clubs: in addition to being active in the UDC, she belonged to more than twenty women's organizations. Daffan was so popular with Texas women that after female suffrage was achieved, they asked her to run for governor. She briefly placed her name on the Democratic primary ballot but removed it for fear of splitting the ticket and enabling a Republican to win.[12]

Farmersville, Collin County

Farmersville is at the intersection of U.S. Highway 380 and State Highway 78. The monument is in City Park, which is between Hill and Main streets.

The twenty-nine members of the Stonewall Jackson Chapter of the UDC raised $2,500 to erect their city's Confederate monument in 1917, an endeavor that took more than five years to complete. Fundraising began in the fall of 1912, when the organization petitioned citizens to pledge amounts ranging from 50 cents to $100 to build a monument. Although more than eighty individual citizens or groups responded to the Daughters' pledge drive, most gave amounts less than $2.50. The old soldiers in the Joseph E. Johnston Camp, UCV, collected $100, the only substantial amount. Placed in City Park, the twenty-five-foot memorial consists of a granite base on top of which stands a life-size figure of a Confederate soldier in regulation uniform with gun at parade rest. The monument, constructed entirely from Texas materials, was dedicated "in memory of all Confederate soldiers."[13] Its inscription is taken from "Recessional," by Rudyard Kipling:

Lord God of hosts be with us yet
Lest we forget, Lest we forget.

Fort Worth, Tarrant County

Fort Worth is at the intersection of interstates 35W, 20, and 30. The monument rests at the head of the Confederate burial plot in Oakwood Cemetery on Grand Avenue and Gould Street.

Despite having had a large and active UDC Chapter since 1897, Fort Worth did not have a single monument to the Confederacy until 1939. The Julia Jackson Chapter tried for many years to raise funds to erect a monument but continually failed. In 1921 the chapter's monument chairperson contacted sculptor Pompeo Coppini, who had achieved national recognition for the monuments he had designed for Texas cities such as Paris and Victoria. The Daughters asked that he send a catalog of designs for memorials ranging from five to twenty thousand dollars, the brochure being a common selling device used by granite dealers at the time. Coppini responded with outrage, claiming that he was an artist and that artists do not have catalogs. A real artist makes each monument individually, said Coppini, because "only such memorials could be a permanent glorification of the deeds of men or nations." He continued, explaining to the monument chairperson that too many artists "compete with the cold blooded and mercenary stone dealers, who love no art and build monuments simply to sell stones."[14]

Coppini did not convince the UDC chapter with his argument, mainly because they simply could not afford to pay for his "artistic" memorials. A few years later the Daughters signed a contract with sculptor Gutzon Borglum. Internationally renowned, Borglum moved to Texas in 1925 to work on a monument to trail drivers that had been commissioned by the Texas Trail Drivers Association. Once again the Julia Jackson Chapter found that they could not raise enough money to purchase the monument, and they broke their contract with Borglum.[15]

In 1938 the chapter finally ordered a monument of white Carrera marble from a granite dealer. The memorial consists of a private wearing an unofficial uniform designed by Mrs. J. J. Nunnally, a longstanding chapter member. The Daughters placed the small figure in the city cemetery, at the head of the section for the R. E. Lee Camp, UCV.[16]

The Julia Jackson Chapter of the UCV remains active today; it funded the monument's restoration in 1991, which was completed by the Anderle Art Factory of Glen Rose, Texas.[17]

Granbury, Hood County

Granbury is thirty-six miles southwest of Fort Worth on U.S. Highway 377. The monument is on the courthouse lawn at the corner of Houston and Bridge streets.

After receiving partial funding from the Texas Legislature, the Gen. Granbury Chapter of the UDC hired Jim Youngblood of the Youngblood Monument Company in Waxahachie to build a pedestal and order a statue from Italy to honor Gen. Hiram B. Granbury. The life-size statue of Granbury is made of granite.[18]

Granbury, a native of Georgia, fought during the Civil War under the command of John Bell Hood and died in 1864, in the Battle of Franklin, Tennessee, where he was buried. In 1893 his family moved his body and reinterred it in the Granbury Cemetery on a small hill overlooking the Hood County seat.[19]

There has been a great deal of debate surrounding the spelling of Granbury's name. His family insists that he spelled his name "Granberry," as it appears on his tombstone, but historians and biographers believe that he went by Granbury.[20]

Greenville, Hunt County

Greenville is sixty miles northeast of Dallas on Interstate 30. The monument is at the corner of Stanford and King streets.

The six-foot granite statue was erected in Greenville by the local UDC chapter and is the only Civil War monument in the state to stand on the grounds of a public school. The Greenville Chapter of the UDC purchased the memorial from the North Texas Marble and Granite Works, a local monument company that served the city's funerary needs. The memorial was dedicated on June 6, 1926, on the grounds of the city's high school. In 1952, when the Greenville High School moved to a new facility, the school board renamed the building Greenville Junior High School; it served the area's youth for another twenty years. The school building was destroyed in the late 1960s to make way for a new post office; at that time the monument was moved to its present location on Stanford and King streets.[21]

The Daughters signed a contract specifying that the monument be built according to a drawing that had been submitted by "the women of the U.D.C.," although the organization's records indicate that a "Mr. Love from Sherman" had sent them a design they liked. Apparently the ladies were not impressed with Mr. Love after meeting him, because it appears that the UDC ordered a premade statue through a catalog from one of the many monument companies in the South selling Confederate statues. The figurative memorial consists of a Confederate soldier at rest atop a small base. The statue is made of blue granite from Winnsboro, South Carolina, while the base is white Victor granite. North Texas Marble and Granite Works completed the memorial, including its concrete base, for $2,660.[22]

Hillsboro, Hill County

Hillsboro is on Interstate 35 at the junction of U.S. highways 81 and 171 and state highways 22 and 171. The monument is on the grounds of the courthouse at the corner of Elm and Covington streets.

Hillsboro erected its monument on July 28, 1925 under the auspices of the Hill County Camp, SCV. Hundreds of county residents descended upon the downtown for the monument ceremony, during which automobiles lined the walkways, and businesses (decorated with red and blue bunting) closed for the celebration. The Hillsboro high school band played a forty-five minute concert while the audience clapped and sang and enjoyed the music. A series of speeches followed, culminating in the monument's unveiling.[23]

The life-size figurative memorial is made of granite from Stone Mountain, Georgia. According to the *Hillsboro Mirror*, the veterans selected this granite for patriotic reasons—it came from the opposite side of the mountain on which the Robert E. Lee memorial was being carved. The Hill County Sons of Confederate Veterans chose Alex Park, the manager of Hillsboro's Monument Works Company, to build the memorial for $5,000.[24]

City leaders planned for the monument unveiling to coincide with the annual reunion of the Old Settlers and Old Soldiers Association. A small occasion by 1925, the reunion was held at the Jefferson Davis State Park grounds just outside of Hillsboro. Long a popular affair in the county with attendances estimated at more than six thousand at the turn of the twentieth century, the reunion had once drawn Texans from across the state who gathered to pay homage to the old veterans while they renewed friendships, ate barbeque and watermelon, and watched their children tear through the carnival midway. By the time the county erected its monument, however, the Hill County Fair had replaced the reunion in importance and only veterans and their immediate families attended the gathering—until the year of the unveiling.[25]

Kaufman, Kaufman County

Kaufman is at the intersection of state highways 34 and 243, and U.S. Highway 175. The monument sits on the courthouse lawn at the corner of Grove and Washington streets.

In 1908, local resident Joseph Huffmaster, in conjunction with the Judah P. Benjamin UCV Camp he commanded, led a campaign to place a larger-than-life-size granite figure of a Confederate soldier on the lawn of the Kaufman County courthouse. Early fundraising efforts proved successful and included camp-sponsored events like the popular "Old Fiddlers' Contest," in which fiddlers competed against each other and then came together at the end of the contest to play the crowds' favorites.[26]

The veterans unveiled the monument on November 22, 1911, a clear, chilly autumn day that encouraged a large crowd. The citizens listened as Kate Daffan, then superintendent of the Confederate Woman's Home in Austin, spoke of the use of "monuments as object lessons in history." She said that Kaufman county had "placed in their midst an object lesson for the heart and memory."[27]

Following the unveiling, the local UDC women served lunch. Local bands played as the veterans' wives sang several songs including, "Under the Flag." Later that evening, the local militia sponsored a mock battle against the old Confederate veterans, one of the earliest Civil War reenactments to occur in Texas. Morris Brothers designed and built the entire monument from a rough block of granite at their monument works in Tyler, Texas. The statue consisted of several bases, each of which was either inscribed or etched with Confederate poetry or figurative representations, such as a pair of army muskets. The monument was dedicated to the name of those men who gave their strength, their undaunted service, and their precious lives. In the name of those women who also served by waiting, watching, weeping, praying, or in their homes made shoes of saddle skirt and blankets of homespun and wove the cloth which clothed themselves and little children. In the name of the Confederate government civil and military, and in the name of one firmly united country and our perpetual flag.[28]

The monument suffered greatly over the years. In 1955 the city removed it to protect it during the construction of a new courthouse. Many citizens were dismayed when it was restored the following year. In an attempt to create symmetry between the monument and the entrance of the new courthouse, the architect had removed the bases, thus shortening the monument. Despite a sizeable protest to restore the monument to its original height, the city commission voted to leave it shortened and the old bases were thrown into a ditch next to the hog pens on the county's poor farm.[29]

Soon after, the restored monument was attacked by vandals, and the sculpted barrel of the gun held by the private soldier atop the monument was lost or stolen and was replaced with a real gun barrel. In 1996 the Kaufman County Historical Commission successfully spearheaded a drive to restore the monument and return it to its original size and condition.[30]

Waxahachie, Ellis County

Waxahachie is at the intersection of Interstate 35E and U.S. Highway 287. The monument sits on the lawn of the courthouse at the corner of Main and Rogers streets.

Waxahachie unveiled its Confederate monument in the middle of the afternoon on a beautiful November day in 1912. A large crowd gathered downtown around the courthouse, in the shadow of the newly constructed Rogers Hotel, which had just been completed at a cost of $100,000. City officials claimed that the hotel was the finest lodging in Ellis County.[31]

In 1911, in an attempt to raise funds for the monument, the Sims-Watson Chapter of the UDC wrote to J. F. Strickland, a local business-

Waxahachie unveiled ITS Confederate monument in 1912 to a large crowd. Courtesy of Ellis County Museum, Waxahachie, Tex.

man and president of the Southern Traction Company, which operated the interurban railway line between Waxahachie and Dallas (thirty miles to the north), and Waco (sixty miles to the south). The Daughters asked Strickland to donate a percentage of the company's gross receipts on sales of fares to the annual Dallas Fair on Confederate's Day. Strickland replied that the company would not be able to set such a precedent as they had connections in several cities and doing so might result in others demanding contributions as well. Instead he promised that he personally would donate for the monument's construction an amount equal to five percent of the company's ticket sales from Waxahachie to the fair on the day of the fair.[32]

With Strickland's donation, the Daughters were able to raise enough money in one year to build and dedicate a Confederate statue on the courthouse lawn. The statue was designed by local resident C.

A. Wilkins, and Waxahachie's granite manufacturer, J. M. Youngblood and Company, built it based on Wilkins's design for $2,500.[33]

Waxahachie's UDC chapter was extremely active at the turn of the twentieth century and twice hosted the Texas Daughters' annual convention. Local resident Margaret Watson served as the organization's state historian for several years; she also compiled a popular book of Civil War songs that sold hundreds of copies.[34]

4.

CENTRAL TEXAS MONUMENTS

Austin, Travis County

AUSTIN IS IN CENTRAL TEXAS along Interstate 35 and is divided by the Colorado River. There are five Civil War monuments in Austin: the *Albert Sidney Johnston Memorial* at the Texas State Cemetery at 3001 Comal Street; the *Austin Confederate Monument*; *Hood's Texas Brigade Monument*, and *Terry's Texas Rangers Memorial*, all on the grounds of the Texas State Capitol; and the *Littlefield Memorial Fountain*, which is dedicated to those University of Texas students who have fought in wars, including the Civil War, and can be found on the South Mall of the University of Texas campus.

Albert Sidney Johnston Memorial

Organized in Austin in 1897, the Albert Sidney Johnston Chapter of the UDC declared that their "grand objective" was to "erect a monument over the grave of Albert Johnston, that gallant commander, who when dying, begged that his body might be laid to rest in Texas soil." Try as they might, the ladies could not raise enough funds to build a suitable memorial, so they petitioned the state organization to help them. Texas UDC president Benedette Tobin organized a monument committee of thirty-four women who presented a petition to the regular session of the Texas legislature in 1898 asking for a state appropriation to build the monument. The legislature denied the UDC's petition. Tobin then increased the committee's membership to fifty and asked Senator R. N. Stafford of Mineola for advice.[1]

Tobin's successor, Eliza Johnson, followed Stafford's advice and organized a media campaign to influence the state legislature. The monument committee sent a copy of the petition to all leading daily newspapers in the state, mailed another 2,600 copies to prominent men in the state, along with a letter asking each of them to sign the petition and send it to the governor. Additionally, the committee sent 200 copies of the petition to UCV camps throughout the state. The UDC tried again in 1901 to secure an appropriation but failed. Undiscouraged, Johnson sent circulars and personal letters to each of Texas's more than 200 legislators and wrote to every newspaper in the state seeking support. During a special session of the legislature in the autumn of 1901, the UDC, "after having first aroused a healthy sentiment over the state for its passage," brought a petition before the House; this time they received a $10,000 appropriation.[2]

Albert Sydney Johnston was a lifetime soldier who graduated from West Point and served in the U.S. Army in the Black Hawk War. In 1836 he moved to Texas, enlisted in the Texas Army, and soon became a senior brigadier general. He was appointed Secretary of War for the Republic of Texas in 1838 and led an expedition against the Cherokees in East Texas the following year. He served as a colonel during the Mexican War and resigned his commission at the beginning of the Civil War to join the Confederate Army. Killed while leading his forces at the Battle of Shiloh, Johnston was originally buried in New Orleans. The Texas Legislature had his remains transferred to Austin in 1867 for reburial. In 1905, noted sculptor Elisabet Ney created a life-size sarcophagus of Italian marble, which the UDC placed over his grave.[3]

Austin Confederate Monument

In 1901 Pompeo Coppini answered Texas granite dealer Frank Teich's call for a sculptor and was immediately put to work on the *Austin Confederate Monument*, funded by the state of Texas and the Camp Hood Confederate Veterans. Teich had already designed the memorial, built the massive granite base, and created four soldiers in granite representing each of the four branches of the Confederate army. Coppini was to create a nine-foot portrait of Confederate President Jefferson Davis in bronze to stand at the top of the memorial. However, when the veterans saw Coppini's figure, they were so pleased that they rejected the four granite soldiers made by Teich's firm and hired Coppini to craft new statues in bronze. This request precipitated a lifelong feud between the two sculptors. Copppini left Teich's employ and began a prolific career, which included sculpting several other Confederate monuments in the state. The *Austin Confederate Monument* consists of five larger-than-life statues in bronze mounted on a fifteen-foot base.[4]

Terry's Texas Rangers Monument

In 1907 Coppini won the commission to create the *Terry's Texas Rangers Monument*, sponsored by the veterans of the Eighth Texas Cavalry. In August 1861, when Benjamin Terry first called for volunteers, more than 1,170 Texas men responded. The all-volunteer regiment served for the duration of the war, surrendering to William Tecumseh Sherman at Greensboro, North Carolina, on April 28, 1865. The surviving veterans of Terry's Rangers organized a committee chaired by Maj. George W. Littlefield with the intent of erecting a monument to honor their fallen comrades. They hired Coppini to create a fourteen-foot equestrian bronze.[5]

Coppini claimed that the monument was the toughest he had undertaken and the project was riddled with problems for the two years he worked on it. Several accidents occurred while the piece was being cast at the John Williams Foundry in New York City, but these problems seemed inconsequential compared to the task of moving the piece to its site on the grounds of the state capitol. After the statue was completed, the county informed Coppini that at 22,000 pounds, the granite base was too heavy to be moved across the Colorado Bridge, which was the most direct route to the capitol. Eventually, Coppini contracted with workmen to wrap the slab with logs and chains and roll it across the riverbed.[6]

Hood's Texas Brigade Monument

Not to be outdone by the veterans of Terry's Texas Rangers, the survivors of Hood's Texas Brigade commissioned a monument to their comrades in 1907. The monument committee chose renowned sculptor Louis Amateis, a Northerner from Washington, D.C., to submit three models from which they would choose their statue. The choice of a Northerner upset several Southern artists, as well as owners of foundries and marble companies. Pompeo Coppini openly criticized the committee for choosing a Yankee, but the chairman replied, "[V]isit your spleen on Mr. Amateis if you like, but do not so approach me again."[7]

Two years later the committee still lacked the necessary funds to start the monument. Reevaluating their position, they hired the McNeel Marble Company of Marietta, Georgia, the largest Civil War monument producer in the South, to create a figurative bronze sculpture on a granite base. Although McNeel was a large distributor of ready-made rather than individualized monuments, their fees were more in line with the brigade's resources.[8]

McNeel built the monument shaft and subcontracted with American Bronze Foundry in Chicago to create the bronze statue. When the piece arrived, the monument committee refused it, claiming that it had several defects. A three-way argument ensued between the committee, the foundry, and McNeel, with McNeel arguing that the piece was of better quality than any of the other statues on the capitol grounds. The committee agreed that the shaft was of good quality and persuaded Pompeo Coppini to quickly sculpt a suitable soldier figure to be cast in bronze and placed at the top of the shaft. Coppini, who had expected to receive the original commission, agreed but on his own terms. He fashioned a heroic-sized Confederate private in a relaxed stance.[9]

The veterans unveiled the monument on October 27, 1910 with an enormous parade. Thousands of veterans attended the ceremonies to hear the speakers: the current governor Texas and a former one, a former Civil War commander of the Trans-Mississippi Department, and one of the state's most successful businessmen. Although most of the speakers praised the bravery and patriotism of Southern soldiers, one of the speakers tried to link the monument to the American Revolution (1776–1783), arguing that the monument was consecrated as a reminder of "American valor, American citizenship, and American patriotism for our comrades who died to preserve and perpetuate the principle upon which this government was founded."[10]

Hood's Texas Brigade served throughout the war, participating in more than two dozen battles. John Bell Hood, its original commander, graduated from the U.S. Military Academy and resigned from the U.S.

Army in 1861 to accept command of the Fourth Texas Infantry. He took command of the Confederate Army of Tennessee in July 1864.[11]

Littlefield Memorial Fountain

In the early 1920s Maj. George W. Littlefield commissioned Coppini to design a Civil War monument for the University of Texas campus. Littlefield, a cattleman, banker, and member of the University's Board of Regents, served during the Civil War in Company I of the Eighth Texas Infantry. Having seen action at Shiloh and Chickamauga, Littlefield returned to Texas in 1863 after being severely wounded in the leg. While the former Confederate officer had hoped to honor his fellow veterans, Coppini asked him to broaden the monument's meaning. Coppini proposed, "why not dedicate your memorial to the boys of the University of Texas who died so that American democracy might spread all over the world, while honoring the leaders you most admire as America's great men?" Littlefield agreed and Coppini set to work designing an allegorical fountain with a female figure, Columbia, surrounded by two male figures at the prow of the ship of state. The ship is guided by nymphs astride three giant sea horses. Coppini's original plans called for six portrait statues of American heroes, three on each side of the fountain centerpiece.[12]

Although Littlefield had approved of Coppini's conception, he died before construction began. By the time the monument was unveiled in 1933, the university regents and architect Paul Cret had changed the original design by placing the statues along the South Mall, leading the viewer's eyes toward the university's Main Building and Tower. Coppini argued that the new installation made his work look like a "dismembered conception," but the university has left the pieces, including the main fountain, where the regents originally placed them.[13]

The six bronze statues along the South Mall include portraits of Albert Sidney Johnston (the oldest piece cast); John H. Reagan, postmaster general of the Confederacy and a Texas statesman; Jefferson Davis, president of the Confederate States of America; James Stephen Hogg, the first native Texan to serve as governor; and Woodrow Wilson, the only twentieth-century figure represented. Coppini claimed that the sixth portrait, a sculpture of Robert E. Lee, was one of his best works. Several years after finishing the fountain he wrote, "I consider the Robert E. Lee the very best portrait statue I ever made of one of my idolized heroes and a great American soldier."[14]

Bastrop, Bastrop County

Bastrop is thirty miles southeast of Austin at the junction of state highways 71, 21, and 95. It sits along the bank of the Colorado River. The city's Confederate monument is on the courthouse lawn at 804 Pine Street.

On October 14, 1910, several hundred people gathered around Bastrop's courthouse singing "America" along with the town's schoolchildren, who had practiced the song for weeks to help celebrate the unveiling of the town's monument to the "Confederate States of America and the Memory of the Confederate soldiers of Bastrop County." There is no indication that community members sensed any irony in celebrating the Confederacy and its soldiers by singing a song in praise of the united nation. By 1910 most Southerners did not consider it incongruous to follow the singing of "America" with a rousing rendition of "Bonnie Blue Flag."[15]

After the crowd quieted, Mrs. E. H. Jenkins, president of the local UDC chapter, addressed the crowd and explained that the sixteen women (eight elderly and eight young) flanking the bunting-wrapped monument represented the "past and the future" of the county. A small girl reached up and pulled the cord to unveil the obelisk of gray Texas granite, which was presented as a "tribute of gratitude of southern women to the devotion and chivalry of southern men," The twenty-seven-foot monument cost $1,800, a sum which had taken the local UDC chapter two years to raise. Depictions of the first and last flags of the Confederacy were carved on the monument's base along with the words "lest we forget." Words from a popular poem are etched on the stone foundation: "Tell it as you may, It never can be told; Sing it as you will, It never can be sung—the story of the glory of the men who wore the gray." (This poem is also carved on the Corsicana monument.)[16]

Belton, Bell County

Belton lies along Interstate 35 at the junction of U.S. highways 81 and 190. The monument is on the courthouse grounds at the corner of

Main Street (State Highway 317) and Central Avenue (State Highway 253).

The Bell County Chapter of the UDC began working to honor county veterans in statuary as soon as it was formed in 1896. After raising the funds to fence Confederate Park, a six-acre tract of land along Nolan Creek that veterans had purchased as the site for their annual reunion, the town's ladies formed a committee to raise money for stone markers to place on the graves of all the county's Confederate soldiers and other men who had aided the Confederate cause. This work occupied the women's club until the mid-1910s, when they began the drive to build a Confederate monument.[17]

Unveiled on December 16, 1916 on the county courthouse lawn, the monument cost $2,500. Local citizens had contributed most of the money, but the largest donation came from Col. J. Z. Miller of Kansas City, Kansas, a former Belton resident. The base and pedestal are made of gray granite, and the Confederate soldier staring out across the lawn is made of marble. On the day of the unveiling a crowd gathered at Tyler School and paraded behind a local band to the square. When they arrived, the band played "Dixie," and two children, Leland Means and Thomas Gordon Saunders—both related to local leading UDC members—led the ceremony. After the children unveiled the monument, Dr. J. C. Hardy, President of nearby Baylor College, addressed the crowd. The ceremony closed with the singing of "God Be With You Till We Meet Again."[18]

Bryan, Brazos County

Bryan is at the intersection of state highways 6 and 21 and U.S. Highway 190. The monument is in the city cemetery on North Texas Avenue (State Highway 6) and Twenty-Fifth Street.

On July 8, 1900 the L. S. Ross Chapter of the UDC erected a square shaft of Italian marble over the grave of Col. Briscoe G. Baldwin, Chief of Ordinance on Gen. Robert E. Lee's staff. Baldwin died in Bryan on September 23, 1898, having moved to Texas after the war. A crowd gathered two years later to honor him and the part he had played in the war. The monument is inscribed with the words of Sir Walter Scott, "Soldier rest, their warfares over. Sleep the sleep that knows no breaking. Dream of battlefields no more, days of danger, nights of waking."[19]

College Station, Brazos County

College Station lies along State Highway 6, south of Bryan at the crossroads of farm-to-market roads 2154, 2347, 2818, and 60. The monument is on the Texas A&M University campus at the entrance to the Academic Building.

On May 4, 1919, the state of Texas and the local UDC chapter honored Lawrence Sullivan Ross with the unveiling of a life-size statue of bronze sculpted by Pompeo Coppini. The Thirty-Fifth Texas Legislature had appropriated funds for the memorial, and contributions also came from the L. S. Ross Chapter of the UDC (named after the war hero) and the J. B. Robertson Camp, UCV. Both organizations consisted of Brazos County citizens, who had collected donations for several years prior to the unveiling. One of the more popular fundraisers held in College Station for the monument was an "Old Folks'" concert. Veteran R. Q. Chatham, the colonel of the veterans' camp, appeared at the front of the "crowded house" at the concert wearing an old Confederate uniform. The crowd cheered enthusiastically and enjoyed an evening of music and singing from the "good old days."[20]

L. S. Ross, or "Sul" as he liked to be called, was a soldier, statesman, and university president. Born in 1838, he immigrated to Texas with his family the following year. By the time he reached college age, Ross had fought in two campaigns against the Comanches. In one of these, the Battle at the Pease River, Ross recaptured Cynthia Ann Parker from the Comanches, much to the celebration of white Texans throughout the state. At the outbreak of the Civil War, Ross joined the Sixth Texas Cavalry and fought at Pea Ridge, Corinth, and Vicksburg. He was promoted to brigadier general in 1864 and commanded Ross's Brigade for the remainder of the war. The brigade saw action in the Atlanta and Franklin-Nashville campaigns.[21]

After the war, Ross farmed near Waco and spent time with his growing family. Within a few years, his neighbors elected him sheriff and shortly thereafter he was nominated to be a delegate to the Constitutional Convention of 1876, and then a representative in the state senate. In 1886 Ross easily won the governorship and served until 1891. Upon leaving office he became president of the Agricultural and Mechanical College of Texas (now Texas A&M University). The college had experienced severe financial problems but Ross ushered in a

The Sul Ross Statue on the Texas A&M Campus. Photograph courtesy of Texas A&M Archives, Texas A&M University.

reign of prosperity. During his tenure enrollment increased, new buildings were built, and public trust in the institution was restored. Ross died suddenly in January 1898, a respected and loved statesman. Sul Ross State University in Alpine is named in his honor.[22]

Each year the newly recruited freshman Corps of Cadets at Texas A&M University polish the Sul Ross monument until it gleams, using only rags and toothbrushes.[23]

Georgetown, Williamson County

Georgetown is north of Austin along Interstate 35. The monument sits on the courthouse lawn on Rock and Eighth streets.

The old Confederate soldiers of Williamson County fell into line that morning in 1916, forming the core of the long parade of citizens who marched the few blocks from the school to the courthouse square in celebration of the unveiling of the town's Confederate monument. As many as five thousand people gathered that day to hear speeches, sing old-time music, and participate in the memorial service. The county judge presiding over the ceremony asserted that the citizens were not gathering "fifty years after the war to take up the ashes of the past" but rather to celebrate the "heroism of the men who endured hardships and incurred dangers for a cause they believed was right." He explained that the citizens were "today loyal to the stars and stripes" but also "loyal to the memory of the stars and bars."[24]

The larger-than-life marble statue portrays a Confederate soldier at parade rest atop a granite obelisk. The monument was funded by the Williamson County Chapter of the UDC and was purchased from the McNeel Marble Company of Georgia from a catalog.[25]

Llano, Llano County

Llano is on State Highway 71, seventy-five miles northwest of Austin. The monument is on the corner of Main (Farm to Market Road 152) and Ford (State Highway 16) streets on the courthouse square.

The Llano County UDC women wanted to build a monument to their county's old soldiers but their fundraising met with "indifference" at first because people thought it "too great an undertaking for the Daughters." The ladies proved them wrong and raised the neces-

sary $1,200 for a monument. Designed by local granite dealer James
K. Finlay, the Daughters unveiled the monument on February 22,
1916, in front of a "crowd estimated to be the largest ever assembled"
in Llano. Texans gathered around the square from counties far
removed from the small rural town, eagerly anticipating Governor
James E. Ferguson's dedication speech. It was reported that they
arrived by "automobile, hack, buggies, and horseback."[26]

The newspaper claimed that "All praise was due the Daughters."
The town cheered as the monument was revealed and the "structure
stood forth in all its splendor, not only as a monument to the Confederates, but to the untiring efforts and ceaseless work of the Daughters
of the Confederacy. They overcame every obstacle, they surmounted
every difficulty."[27]

James K. Finlay and Sons was a longstanding granite dealer and cut-
ter in Llano. Using local granite, the company fashioned many memorials that still stand today. The figurative, larger-than-life Confederate
soldier that stands on Llano's courthouse grounds was created by Finlay's sons, Jack and James, and carved in the likeness of their father. J.
K. Finlay was a pioneer in the Texas granite industry. He began working in 1888, not far from Llano, using a crude polisher consisting of a
rubber wheel that rubbed sand against stone. Finlay had produced
many of the columns in the state capitol building in Austin, having
spent three weeks polishing a single pillar. He and his sons established
the cutting and finishing plant in Llano after the turn of the century
and provided granite work of high quality to Texans.[28]

Marlin, Falls County

Marlin is at the intersection of state highways 6 and 7, thirty miles
southeast of Waco. The monument sits on the courthouse grounds at
the intersection of Bridge (State Highway 7) and Fortune streets.

The John M. Jolly Chapter of the UDC tried for several years to
raise funds to create a Civil War memorial in their community, but was
unable to generate enough money. Mrs. B. C. Clark, a Daughter from
the chapter in Rosebud, Texas, intervened and provided the remaining
amount needed to order a statue. The Jolly Chapter, named in honor
of local veteran and prominent citizen, John M. Jolly, purchased a
drinking fountain and placed it on the courthouse lawn. The fountain

is inscribed with the phrase, "a token of appreciation to the valor and sacrifice of the Confederate soldiers, 1925."[29]

That same year, the UDC in Marlin erected a memorial cabin on the courthouse grounds. The cabin was constructed out of logs from several pioneer-built houses that were falling into ruin. It proved to be a favorite gathering place, especially for meetings of the local Boy and Girl Scouts. In the late 1920s, when renovations were being made on the courthouse, the log cabin provided temporary office space for court personnel.[30]

Marlin is most famous for its hot mineral waters. Discovered in 1892, the waters were used for healing practices and became the foundation of economic activity in the community.

Several large baths, a general hospital, and a hospital for crippled children were built. Marlin remained popular as a place to "take the waters" until after World War II.[31]

Temple, Bell County

Temple lies along Interstate 35 at the intersection of state highways 53 and 95, thirty-six miles south of Waco. The monument sits on the north side of Hillcrest Cemetery, in Section A, at 1601 North Main Street. Called Hillcrest Cemetery since the 1920s, its legal name is the Temple Cemetery Company.

The monument's granite shaft is made of Georgia marble, donated jointly by the Lavenia Porter Talley Chapter of the UDC and the Granbury Camp, UCV. Area citizens unveiled the monument in June 1910, placing it among the graves of both Confederate and Union soldiers. The shaft is inscribed with a section of a poem by Father Ryan:

> "we care not whence they come,
> dead in lifeless clay;
> their cause and country still the same;
> they died and wore the gray."[32]

Many Americans considered Father Abram J. Ryan the poet laureate of the Confederacy and the Lost Cause movement. He was the most popular poet working in the South during the decades after the war, and his most famous poem was *The Conquered Banner*. Having been a chaplain in the Confederate Army, Ryan spent the rest of his life seeking words to describe his wartime experiences and express his belief in the rightness of the Southern cause. Although he only wrote poetry part-time, he published 937 poems. To earn a living, Ryan edited several prominent Southern newspapers and a magazine. He also served as a pastor at the Saint Mary Church in Mobile, Alabama, for more than a decade prior to his death. Many monuments across the South are engraved with phrases from Ryan's poems.[33]

Waco, McClellan County

Waco is on Interstate 35, seventy miles south of Dallas. The monument is in Oakwood Cemetery on South Fifth Street.

Shortly after noon on May 2, 1893, the Pat Cleburne and China Spring Camps of the UCV; the Baylor Cadets, teachers, and students; the Waco Light Guards; and a host of citizens and schoolchildren gathered in front of the main building on the Baylor University campus and marched to Oakwood Cemetery. It was Decoration Day, the day set aside to mark the graves with flowers, but in 1893 the somber celebration had another purpose. Veterans of the Pat Cleburne Camp planned to unveil a monument to their comrades.[34]

As the first monument erected in tribute to the Confederacy in Texas, the granite obelisk marked the graves of forty veterans and their wives, including a few unnamed plots. The simple shaft bears the inscription, "In memory of the brave men and devoted women of the South."[35]

The unveiling ceremony began at three o'clock in the afternoon with prayer and music, followed by a short address by veteran J. D. Shaw. After the speech, Rosa King, the teenage daughter of a veteran, read a poem written by her mother. The Waco newspaper applauded her effort, claiming that she had recently received lessons in elocution while visiting friends in Washington, D.C. The Commander General of the Trans-Mississippi Department, W. L. Cabell, who lived in Dallas, attended the ceremony, eager to take part in the first unveiling of a Civil War monument in the state.[36]

5.

THE PANHANDLE AND WEST TEXAS MONUMENTS

Amarillo, Potter County

AMARILLO IS IN THE TEXAS PANHANDLE at the junction of U.S. Highway 287 and Interstate 40. The monument is in Ellwood Park on West Eleventh and Adams streets.

Four elderly and stooped veterans gathered in Ellwood Park on June 8, 1931, to be honored at a monument-unveiling ceremony as the last living Confederate soldiers in the area. The monument, erected by the Will A. Miller Chapter of the UDC, was made out of Vermont and Italian marble and had been ordered from H. A. Whitacre, a monument maker in New York. Whitacre had shipped the granite shaft and marble soldier to the dusty Panhandle town where the Osgood Memorial Company, a local monument business, set the statue in place.[1]

On the day of the unveiling, hundreds of local citizens gathered in Ellwood Park. The children ran among the trees, most of which were young saplings recently planted on what had once been grassy prairie land. A wind blew from the south, whipping dust into the eyes of the participants, but few people minded as they reveled in the Municipal Band's playing and waited to hear speeches from Georgia Kirkman, president of the local UDC chapter, Mayor Ernest O. Thompson, and State Congressman Marvin Jones.[2]

El Paso, El Paso County

El Paso lies at the far western tip of Texas where New Mexico and the Mexican state of Chihuahua meet along Interstate 10. The monument is in Evergreen Cemetery at 4301 Alameda.

Amarillo's Confederate monument. Author photograph.

On September 18, 1919, the Robert E. Lee Chapter of the UDC and the John C. Brown Chapter of Confederate Veterans unveiled the monument in Evergreen Cemetery to their community's war dead. The memorial shaft sits among the graves of forty Confederate veterans, a few Confederate widows, and a handful of fallen World War I veterans, including the grave of Lindley Spencer, one of the first El Pasoans to die (in 1917) in World War I. The UDC originally purchased the burial plot in 1908 when the women learned of a Confederate who was dying in a South El Paso hovel. Intending to commemorate the city's war dead after the upheaval of World War I, the Daughters were determined to create a monument that would mark the graves of both Confederate and World War I veterans.[3]

The front of the monument bears the simple inscription, "Our Confederate Dead" and the back bears the dual inscription, "Our men who died for Liberty, 1917–1918" and "1941–1946," the latter having been added by the Daughters in 1949.[4]

Lubbock, Lubbock County

The largest city on Texas's southern plains, Lubbock lies on Interstate 27, more than 300 miles northwest of Dallas and 120 miles south of Amarillo. The monument sits on the courthouse grounds on Broadway Street.

A small and simple granite stone on the courthouse lawn states that Lubbock County was "named for a Texas Confederate." Thomas (or Thompson, as some sources claim) Saltus Lubbock was indeed a Texas Confederate and a hard-line secessionist. After shots were fired at Fort Sumter, he and a handful of other men converged on the Confederate capital to petition Jefferson Davis for the authority to "raise a company or battalion of guerrillas." Shortly after the Battle of First Manassas, Lubbock returned to Texas and recruited, along with his close friend Benjamin Terry, the Eighth Texas Cavalry, more commonly known as Terry's Texas Rangers. Terry served as regimental colonel and Lubbock as lieutenant colonel. In poor health, Lubbock abandoned the regiment in Nashville in late 1861, and died a few months later.[5]

As the monument inscription states, Lubbock was both a Texas Confederate and a Texas Ranger who led men against the Mexican

Army during the Texas Revolution. Lubbock had originally been drawn to the state as part of a company of New Orleans Greys, participating first in the siege of Bexar and then in the Texan Santa Fe expedition, during which he was captured in New Mexico and escaped back to Texas by jumping from a second-story window. Lubbock ended his career in the Texas Revolution by leading the drive to push the Mexicans back across the Rio Grande after the seizure of San Antonio in 1842. He and 188 other men marched back to Texas, declining to join William S. Fisher and his ill-fated Mier Expedition.[6]

Memphis, Hall County

Memphis lies at the junction of U.S. Highway 287, State Highway 256, and Farm to Market Road 1547. The monument sits on the courthouse square on Noel (State Highway 256) and Fifth streets.

The Winnie Davis Chapter of the UDC, American Legion Post 175, and the American Legion Auxiliary worked together to erect the life-size figurative monument that sits on the courthouse grounds in Memphis. Unveiled on March 18, 1924, *Our Patriots* honors Confederate and World War I veterans. The monument has a central shaft with two soldiers on it: one a Confederate standing at parade rest, and the other, a doughboy, at attention. The names of the county's soldiers are inscribed on the base.[7]

The Daughters began raising funds for a monument prior to World War I, but they simply could not gather enough donations. Even with the help of World War I veterans and their wives, the monument committee found itself short of money and unable to make the payments on the monument in the months prior to the unveiling. In a last push, the club members asked every citizen of Hall County to contribute a small amount to cover the $2,000 cost of the memorial. The drive was successful, and the monument's creators were finally able to pay for the statue.[8]

On the afternoon of the unveiling, area citizens crowded onto the courthouse lawn. An estimated 3,000 Texans had turned out to see the monument and listen to the speakers. Schoolchildren ran wildly, as most rural schools in the county had dismissed their students for the day and encouraged parents to take the children to the county seat to witness the historical event. Led by the Chamber of Commerce band, a parade of veterans and others formed at city hall. The procession snaked through the city streets and ended at the courthouse, where Memphis honored both old Confederates and World War I veterans. After an address on "Our Confederate Soldiers," the band played "Dixie" and the few elderly veterans in gray stood up and let out a rousing rebel yell. There were additional speeches by women from both the UDC and the Ladies Legion Auxiliary, followed by more music.[9]

G. W. Backus designed the memorial. Backus owned and operated the Backus Monument Company, also known as Thittle Works, in the nearby town of Vernon. Although the company has experienced several changes in ownership, it still operates today at its original location on Wilbarger Street. Every few years, as more veterans passed away, Backus or an associate would add their names to the list of Hall County veterans on the monument's plaques. In 1986 the citizens of Memphis rededicated the monument to honor all the county's war veterans by placing a stone slab at the base of the memorial that reads, "In memory of all veterans of all wars."[10]

Vernon, Wilbarger County
Vernon is at the intersection of U.S. Highways 70, 183, 283, and 287, some fifty miles northwest of Wichita Falls. The monument sits on the courthouse lawn on Wilbarger (U.S. Highway 287) and Main (U.S. Highway 283) streets.

Unveiled on April 23, 1916, the life-size statue of a Confederate soldier stands at parade rest atop the large shaft and gazes across the courthouse grounds. The shaft is engraved with the phrase, "In honor of those who fought and died, of those who fought and lived." The Lawrence S. Ross Chapter of the UDC likely ordered the $750 monument from local granite dealer G. W. Backus of Backus Monument Company.[11]

Wichita Falls, Wichita County
Wichita Falls is on U.S. Highways 287, 82, and 277 and Interstate 44, two hours northeast of Fort Worth. The monument is at the W. I. Memorial Auditorium, now the town's city hall, at the corner of Seventh and Bluff streets.

The W. R. Scurry Chapter of the UDC unveiled their Confederate monument in 1934, "in memory of the sons of the Southland." The Daughters intended the monument to serve as a history lesson for the citizens of Wichita Falls, inscribing on one side of the simple obelisk the phrase, "Let this mute but eloquent structure speak to generations to come of a generation of the past."[12]

The Daughters named their chapter in honor of William R. Scurry, who moved to Texas in 1837 and joined the army in 1846 as a private to fight in the Mexican-American War. Scurry distinguished himself in battle, and when the Civil War began, he enlisted once again. Soon promoted to major, Scurry eventually rose to the rank of brigadier general, fighting in New Mexico at the battles of Glorieta Pass and Val Verde. With the Union victory at Glorieta Pass and Confederate movements in the Southwest effectively ended, Scurry was reassigned to Walker's Texas Division and fought in Arkansas and Louisiana. Scurry was killed in 1864 at the Battle of Sabine Pass.[13]

The Victoria Chapter, UCV, also memorialized Scurry by naming their chapter after him. Scurry County in West Texas bears the name of the Confederate hero.[14]

In 1936 the Daughters placed a small marker on the grave of W. R. Scurry's son, Judge Edgar Scurry, a longtime resident and esteemed citizen of Wichita Falls. Judge Scurry had served in the local Sons of Confederate Veterans organization and had helped the Daughters to form their chapter in 1912. Scurry's marker and grave can be found in Riverside Cemetery.[15]

6.
SOUTH TEXAS MONUMENTS

Brownsville, Cameron County

BROWNSVILLE IS AT THE SOUTHERNMOST TIP of Texas across from Matamoras, Mexico, and is the southern terminus of U.S. highways 77 and 83. The monument is on International Boulevard (State Highway 4), on the corner of East Tyler and East Ninth streets.

The national UDC dedicated a small gray boulder to Jefferson Davis in 1926. The memorial, made of granite from Llano, Texas, marks an intersection of the Jefferson Davis Highway and honors the only president of the Confederacy and his service to the U.S. Army in Mexico.[1]

Davis held the position of colonel during the Mexican-American War and landed troops at Point Isabel, marching his men into the interior of the country. The Daughters claimed he was the hero of the Battles of Buena Vista and Monterey.[2]

The monument sits not far from the scene of the Battle of Palmito Ranch, the last battle of the Civil War, which took place in March 1865. In this battle, the 62nd U.S. Colored Infantry fired the last volley of the Civil War while in retreat from advancing Confederate forces. Private John J. Williams of Indiana was the only man killed in the battle; he was also the last man to die in the Civil War.[3]

Comfort, Kendall County

Comfort lies at the junction of State Highway 27, U.S. Highway 87, and Interstate 10 about fifty miles northwest of San Antonio. The monument is on High Street two blocks from State Highway 27 on a hillside across from the city's old high school campus.

In the late 1850s, much of the Hill Country's population consisted of first- and second-generation German immigrants. Although many of these new citizens had adapted to local ways—for example, some held slaves and planted cotton—others refused to follow their fellow Anglo Texans down the road to secession. Some German communities in the state remained loyal to the Union, despite great suffering and hardships, and in 1862, an estimated sixty-five of the men from Comfort and the surrounding area left Texas and went to Mexico rather than be drafted into the Confederate army. The men believed that they would either wait out the war in Mexico or find a way to join with Union forces.[4]

The small cadre of German American men encamped along the banks of the Nueces River, about twenty miles from Fort Clark in Kinney County. At dawn on August 10, 1862, the men were surprised by mounted Confederate soldiers. In the ensuing battle, known as the Battle of the Nueces, nineteen of the German Unionists were killed. Nine more were wounded, and the Confederates executed these men a few hours after the battle. The unharmed German American Unionists tried to escape. In October, Confederate soldiers caught and killed eight of them crossing the Mexican border. A few managed to get back into Texas while another handful headed north to California. Eleven of the men returned to the Comfort area, telling their friends and families about the slaughter. Eventually a few of the survivors managed to join Union forces headquartered in New Orleans.[5]

There are several conflicting contemporary and eyewitness accounts of the battle, especially in regard to the number of men involved in the fighting and the number of casualties, but survivors of the battle were sure of one thing, the need to gather their dead and return them home to Comfort.[6]

After the Civil War ended, seventeen men from Comfort traveled to the battle site, gathered two sacks of their comrades' bones, interred them on a bluff outside the little town, and erected a monument to honor their sacrifice. The granite obelisk, *Treue Der Union*, is the only foreign-language memorial to the Civil War in Texas and one of only three memorials to the Union in the state. Erected on August 10, 1866, four years to the day after the Battle of the Nueces, *Treue Der Union* is the first monument dedicated to the Civil War in Texas.[7]

The Comfort Heritage Foundation restored the monument in 1994, under the supervision of master stonemason Karl H. Kuhn from the nearby town of Boerne.[8]

Corpus Christi, Nueces County

Corpus Christi is on Interstate 37 and U.S. Highways 77 and 181, some 210 miles southwest of Houston on the Gulf of Mexico. The monument is at the Broadway Bluff Balustrade at the end of Schatzell and Peoples streets.

The women of the Corpus Christi Chapter of the UDC pulled their wraps closely around them. The wind, blowing from the sea and across the newly created balustrade, whipped at their long, flared skirts, but the ladies persevered, watching as the townspeople gathered for the unveiling of the first public outdoor art in Corpus.[9]

Although the work of placing a piece of art in the city had begun many years before by a different women's organization, the Daughters prided themselves on having brought the task to completion. They contracted with Pompeo Coppini to create *Queen of the Sea*, which the city revealed in 1915 to hundreds of people. The ceremonies included the usual speeches and songs, and as an added treat, city officials hired an opera singer to thrill the crowd with the "Star Spangled Banner."[10]

Inspired by a walk along the beach, Coppini claimed that he had wanted to create something radically different from the "stereotypical memorial" to the Confederacy. He imagined a piece of sculpture that would represent the reunited South and North and the passion of the people of Corpus Christi for their beautiful city. He wrote later that the "fountain portrays heroic allegorical figures which tell in true artistic language, of the meeting of the two elements (land and sea), and the rich gifts which they bring to the city lying between." The semicircular piece has Mother Earth on one side and Father Neptune on the other, joining hands over the head of a young maiden. At their feet lie the trophies of the sea and land, a visual representation of their resources and riches.[11]

Although Coppini wanted to cast the piece in bronze, the Daughters chose to use imitation granite, largely because of budgetary constraints. One of Coppini's students, Aldine Touch, had completed a monument in San Antonio made of the same material, and the UDC believed it would serve their purpose. The Daughters had used "every means of turning an honest penny," including holding rummage sales, waffle suppers, and working as clerks on special sale days at a local furniture store for a percentage of the profits but managed to raise only $1,000, including the money that the men's Rotarian Club had raised in their fundraising drive. Despite the small sum, Coppini agreed to create the statue and gave the city his labor as a gift, charging only for materials.[12]

Seventy-five years later, one of the young women who had attended the original unveiling donned her best dress and stood on the balustrade once more as the sea air refreshed another large crowd. The ceremony revealed a newly restored *Queen of the Sea*, paid for by the Rotary Club. Art professor Ron Sullivan of nearby Del Mar College did the reconstruction work. Once again music entertained the crowd and speakers extolled the history of the monument. Ellana Cochran, the woman who attended both unveilings, told reporters that she was fourteen years old when the monument was first unveiled, and that she had carried on for weeks afterward, imitating the opera singer. Looking affectionately at the monument so many years later, Cochran expressed the enthusiasm that Corpus Christi's citizens feel toward the monument when she said, "I love it."[13]

Gonzales, Gonzales County

Gonzales lies along U.S. highways 90, 97, and 183. The monument sits in Confederate Heroes Square, downtown at the corner of St. Louis and St. Paul streets.

When Gonzales unveiled its marble memorial in June 1909, it claimed to be the smallest town in Texas to erect a monument to the Confederacy. Although only 5,000 people lived in the town at the time, the Gonzales Chapter of the UDC had raised more than $3,700 over five years. They hired Frank Teich of Llano to design the life-size sculpture of a Confederate soldier on picket duty. The twelve-foot-square base of the memorial reaches a height of forty feet. At the time it was unveiled, granite curbing and an iron fence surrounded the monument.[14]

Mrs. B. B. Hoskins, president of the city's UDC chapter and the individual responsible for initiating the monument's creation, delivered one of the main addresses on the day of its unveiling. "Could our heart's wish have been gratified," she called out from the podium to the crowd, "this Confederate monument would have been made of burnished gold, studded with precious stones, and would reach as high as the heavens."[15]

New Braunfels, Comal County

New Braunfels sits along Interstate 35 at the intersection of Farm to Market Road 725. The city is thirty miles south of San Antonio and forty-five miles southwest of Austin. The monument is on the corner of East San Antonio and Seguin avenues in the main plaza downtown.

Maj. Ira Cohee, a chaplain from nearby Fort Sam Houston, spoke at the unveiling ceremony, praising local businessman Ernest A. Clousnitzer and his gift to the city. The monument was dedicated to "The memory of our fallen soldiers, 1861–1865," and Cohee marveled at the city's spirit for consecrating a memorial to the dead of both North and South. The New Braunfels monument is the only memorial in Texas dedicated to both the Confederacy and the Union, although it is not surprising that this small German community honored both sides—many Germans supported the United States during the war, and some enlisted and fought for the North. But another group of at least 300 German American men led by a local German, Gustav V. Hoffmann, enlisted in the Confederacy.[16]

Ernest Clousnitzer purchased the white marble statue of a Confederate soldier standing at ease with a rifle in hand from the city of Jacksonville, Texas. The East Texas town had contracted to buy the statue (more than likely from Frank Teich) but found itself short of funds and unable to pay for it. Clousnitzer bought the statue and gave it to the city of New Braunsfels as a gift in March 1935. The American Legion and its Ladies Auxiliary planned the unveiling ceremony and invited as honored guests the only living Civil War veterans in the area—Gottlieb Zipp (age 90) and his brother William Zipp (age 91). Prominent local men gave speeches and the women of the Ladies Auxiliary of the Comal Post American Legion sang "America."[17]

In addition to the Civil War monument, Clousnitzer donated a second statue, *Spirit of the American Doughboy*, to the city. Dedicated on Armistice Day, November 11, 1937, the memorial honored the county's World War I veterans and was created by sculptor E. M. Viquesney of Indiana. Clousnitzer owned the Citizens Ice Company, originally founded in 1925 as the Citizens Ice and Ice Cream Company. He died in 1941, but his business continued to operate at 262 West Jahn Street until 1961.[18]

In 2001 the Sons of Confederate Veterans held a raffle to pay for replacing the rifle carried by the soldier statue. They purchased an original Confederate Enfield, which a sculptor would use to create a mold for casting a replacement of the original gun; after the mold was made, the Enfield would be raffled off to pay for the new casting. The repair cost $2,000. The Sons of Confederate Veterans appear to have assumed that the statue honored only Confederate soldiers, referring to the monument as a "Johnny Rebel." They may have assumed this because the state of Texas had placed a historical marker near the monument stating the number of men from Comal County who had volunteered to defend the Confederacy. But in 1935, both Clousnitzer and the citizens of New Braunfels's had intended the monument to represent far more than just one side of the conflict—they meant for the monument to honor all the men who gave their lives in the struggle.[19]

San Antonio, Bexar County

San Antonio lies along Interstate 10 at the junction of interstates 35 and 37. The monument is in Travis Park, at the corner of Travis and Navarro streets.

Mrs. A. W. Houston stepped out onto the front porch. Milling about on her lawn and in the street in front of her home were members of the Bernard E. Bee Chapter of the UDC and local Confederate veterans. They came to attention as Houston welcomed them and asked if they were ready to march. Houston took her place at the front of the procession and led the group down the street to Travis Park, a small green area in downtown San Antonio named for William B. Travis, defender of the Alamo.[20]

A large crowd had already gathered in the park, and Houston led the Daughters and veterans through the crowd to a roped-off area near the monument. Three years in the planning, San Antonio's first piece of public art was unveiled on April 28, 1900, and Mrs. A. W. Houston was responsible for its creation. As the first and only president of the local UDC chapter, she had persuaded her organization to begin raising funds, and when the possibility of a memorial appeared to be a reality, she contacted the daughter of one of the members, Virginia Montgomery—an artist living in New Orleans—to design the memorial.[21]

Montgomery donated a plan for the monument that consisted of a larger-than-life-size Confederate soldier of Llano granite standing with his right fist raised and his finger pointing upward because, as the Montgomery explained, "he leaves all to the God of battles and dispenser of justice." The monument is inscribed with the phrase, "let we forget" (from Rudyard Kipling's poem, "Recessional") and a second, "our cause is with God." San Antonio's UDC chapter hailed the monument as the first piece of Confederate public art commissioned and designed by a Southern woman in the United States (there were other women sculptors working and receiving commissions at the time, most notably Elizabeth Ney in Texas, but Montgomery defined herself as the first Southern woman to design a Confederate monument, and it is likely that she was).[22]

Texas granite dealer Frank Teich followed Montgomery's design when he sculpted the shaft and soldier out of granite from his factory in Llano. Teich had built a home in San Antonio in the early 1880s and established a shop at the corner of Alamo Street and Aransas Pass Railroad track to promote his business. As one of the earliest Confederate monuments erected in the state, San Antonio's memorial has suffered its share of vandalism. During the 1960s, local businesses lobbied to dig up Travis Park and move the monument elsewhere to make way for a large parking garage. Local history buffs and members of the UDC and SCV organizations came out in full force, determined to save the park and the monument. After a bitter fight, the park remained and Montgomery's Confederate still stands tall, its finger pointing heavenward.[23]

Victoria, Victoria County

Victoria sits at the convergence of U.S. highways 59, 77, and 89. The monument is south of downtown at De Leon Plaza.

Sculptor Pompeo Coppini stooped over the letter he was writing,

Pompeo Coppini's masterpiece *The Last Stand*. Courtesy of University of Houston–Victoria.

detailing his plans for Victoria's Confederate monument. "My conception is of a hero standing after a hard battle," he explained, "wounded at the edge of a cliff commanding the enemy's camp, awaiting for [*sic*] a new desperate attack." Glancing up, Coppini could see the sculpture's form in his mind and bowing his head once more he wrote, "I have been almost forced to immortalize our heroes in a dress parade costume, as if the future generations would care to remember them as a horde of well fed, easy going members of a regular army in time of peace."[24]

The William P. Rogers Chapter of the UDC embraced Coppini's plans, unveiling one of the most unusual and original pieces of Civil War commemoration art in Texas. Dubbed *The Last Stand*, Victoria's bronze monument stands ten feet tall, excluding its massive red granite base. In 1894, local women formed an association whose purpose was to earn funds to erect a memorial. Two years later, a sizable number of its members also formed the Rogers Chapter of UDC, and in 1900 the two organizations merged and combined their funds. Still, the Daughters struggled for many years to raise enough money to build a monument.[25]

June 3, 1912, dawned warm with a smell of anticipation in the air. The much-awaited monument was to be unveiled finally. An entirely female committee planned an elaborate program that included a parade consisting of local veterans, their daughters and sons, and in honor of the reconciliation between the states, the Wagner Silver Cornet Band of the Grand Army of the Republic.[26]

An estimated two thousand citizens gathered for the speeches and music at the Public Square, later renamed De Leon Plaza, eager to see the monument that Coppini claimed to be his "masterpiece." Coppini stood among the crowd, watching the public's response to the monument, which had been cast at the Roman Bronze Works in New York for $5,000.[27]

Katie Wheeler, the young daughter of the recently deceased president of the Roger Chapter of the UDC, pulled the cord, revealing the monument. In hushed whispers the crowd stretched for a better view. "What did the monument stand for?" asked one of the male speakers at the ceremony. Answering his own question he said, "it stood for the memory of the men who gave their lives, their fortunes, their every hope in defense of their homes, firesides, and for a cause that was dearer than all else on earth to them."[28]

7.

SOUTHEAST TEXAS MONUMENTS

Alvin, Brazoria County

ALVIN IS TWELVE MILES SOUTHEAST OF HOUSTON at the junction of state highways 6 and 35. The monument is in the Confederate Cemetery on Farm to Market Road 517 near the intersection of State Highway 35.

The Lamar Fontaine Chapter of the UDC dedicated a monument to the John A. Wharton Camp, UCV, on May 30, 1924. The old soldiers had named their camp in honor of Wharton, a Confederate brigadier general from Brazoria County. The monument is inscribed with the phrase "superior to adversity; equal to prosperity."[1]

In the 1890s veterans in the county purchased a plot of land, named it Confederate Cemetery, and dedicated it as the final resting place for local veterans and their families. With the large numbers of deaths following the hurricane of 1900, they increased the cemetery's acreage and opened the grounds to nonveteran dead. Several hurricane victims are also buried in the cemetery. Although most Americans rightly associate the hurricane of 1900 with Galveston, the fierce storm destroyed towns across the Texas gulf region as well, leaving death and destruction in its wake. Today, the dead from all of the last four American wars are buried in the cemetery, along with several civic leaders.[2]

Bay City, Matagorda County

Bay City is at the junction of State Highways 35 and 60, ninety miles southwest of Houston. The monument is on the corner of Seventh Street (State Highway 35) and Avenue F (State Highway 60), on the town square.

Given to the city by the E. S. Rugeley Chapter of the UDC and funded largely by Mrs. E. S. Rugeley, the chapter's lifetime president, Bay City's monument stands over twenty-eight feet tall and is crowned by a life-size figure of a Confederate soldier at rest. Made of Italian marble, the soldier tops a shaft of Georgia marble designed by the McNeel Marble Company of Marietta, Georgia, one of the largest distributors of monuments in the South after the Civil War. The cost of the monument was $2,750.[3]

On a cold but clear January morning in 1913, more than 3,000 area citizens gathered around the courthouse square to watch the elderly Confederate veterans parade to the site of the monument unveiling. The small UDC chapter of fifty-three dedicated women led the ceremonies, and Mrs. Rugeley spoke of the "memory of our Confederate soldiers."[4]

Many years later, the Rugeley Chapter placed a small memorial shaft in Matagorda Cemetery to honor the twenty-two men who had frozen or drowned defending nearby Matagorda Island in November and December 1863, prior to its abandonment and eventual takeover by Union troops.[5]

Beaumont, Jefferson County
Beaumont is on Interstate 10, eighty-five miles east of Houston. The monument is in Weiss Park at the corner of Laurel and Magnolia streets.

Miss Eddie Kuhn looked nervously over the crowd that had gathered for the annual Confederate Day celebration at the Southeast Texas Fair. She cleared her throat and said, "We as granddaughters of Confederate soldiers now unveil to your view this monument, erected in memory of those whose valor and achievements will live in history while patriotism and civilization endure."[6]

Kuhn's speech culminated the drive to erect a monument in Beaumont. Funded by the Albert Sidney Johnston Camp, UCV, and the citizens of Beaumont, the cast bronze figure of a Confederate private standing at parade rest was purchased from the McNeel Marble Company of Marietta, Georgia. The life-size figure stands atop a marble shaft dedicated to "our Confederate soldiers rendered immortal by his [*sic*] deeds of valor, sacrifices, and achievements, 1861–1865, which are without a parallel in history."[7]

The old soldiers led the parade to Keith Park, in the heart of the city, for the unveiling ceremony. The Confederates marched in front of their former enemies, represented by local veterans of the Grand Army of the Republic, the vanquished leading the victors to memorialize the war. Decorated floats followed the soldiers, each carrying one of thirteen young girls who represented the former thirteen Confederate states. The local UDC chapter marched behind the floats, followed by more than 1,000 schoolchildren who, having been dismissed from school for the day, were happily waving Confederate flags.[8]

Newspaper reports and the *Confederate Veteran*, the official magazine for most Confederate organizations, wrote that the monument was cast in bronze, and it is likely that the veterans who purchased the sculpture assumed it was bronze, but a restoration in the late 1980s proved otherwise. The figure of the soldier, having fallen as a result of a severe storm in October 1986, underwent extensive repairs carried out by Weeren Enterprises, Inc. The company discovered that the soldier was actually made of molded copper.[9]

Although the veterans originally placed the monument in the city center in Keith Park (also known as City Park), in 1926 city leaders petitioned to move it to another, less centrally located park.[10]

Galveston, Galveston County

Galveston Island lies two miles offshore in the Gulf of Mexico. The southern terminus of Interstate 45, Galveston is 50 miles south of Houston. The city's main monument stands on the lawn of the County Courthouse, formerly the heart of Central Park, on Broadway Avenue (U.S. Highway 75 and Texas Highway 87). A second smaller monument is in the Episcopal Cemetery.[11]

Erected on June 3, 1911 under the auspices of the local UDC chapter, though largely paid for by the organization's lifetime president, Mollie R. Magill Rosenberg, *Dignified Resignation* was unveiled in the heart of the city's main park. The larger-than-life-size bronze Confederate figure towers more than twenty feet high, representing "a typical southern soldier, torn battle flag crossed to his breast and in the right hand, a broken sword." The statue's base is made of granite.[12]

Rosenberg's name is prominently inscribed on the base, as are the

Galveston's monument, *Dignified Resignation*. Author photograph.

names of the three women who formed the monument committee. The memorial is inscribed with these words: "there has never been an armed force which in purity of motives, intensity of courage and heroism has equaled the army and navy of the C. S. of A."

Molly Rosenberg and her husband Henry were prominent and wealthy citizens of Galveston. Henry had been involved in numerous charitable organizations and provided in his will for the funding of one of the city's first pieces of public art. That monument, commemorating the Texas Revolution of 1836, was erected in 1900, months after Henry's death. It sits at the intersection of Rosenberg Avenue and Broadway. Galveston's *Texas Independence* monument was also unveiled before a large crowd—an estimated 10,000 locals—and a parade highlighted the events while a choir of schoolchildren sang patriotic songs.[13]

Several years later, enjoying her large inheritance and the freedom of widowhood, Molly Rosenberg donated the Confederate monument, meant to be a reminder of the South's sacrifices, and more personally, of her own youth in war-torn Virginia, where she had witnessed the horrors of the war in a soldier's hospital.[14]

Houston, Harris County

Houston, the fourth largest city in the United States, is at the junction of interstates 10 and 45. The city has two Confederate monuments: the *Spirit of the Confederacy* in Sam Houston Park at 1100 Bagby, and the Dick Dowling monument in Hermann Park, on Outer Belt Drive at Brailsfort.

Urged on by their parents, the children gathered around the monument. The hundreds of youngsters assembled played a prominent role in the unveiling ceremonies of the Dick Dowling monument, funded by the Dick Dowling Camp, UCV, and a host of Irish societies. As more adults began to assemble around Market Square, near City Hall, ceremony leaders signaled the children to begin singing. They enchanted the crowd with patriotic tunes and old Southern folk songs like "In My Old Kentucky Home." The audience, energized by the children's voices, joined in and soon thousands were singing and enjoying the day's festivities.[15]

Planned to coincide with St. Patrick's Day, the unveiling of the

Dowling monument sparked a frenzy of green in the city, and the newspapers reported that "everyone was Irish" on March 17, 1905, as the city celebrated the Irish-born Confederate hero, Richard "Dick" Dowling. Designed by Frank Teich of Llano, the larger-than-life-size portrait of Dowling in Italian marble commemorates both the leader and the force of forty-three soldiers he led. Dowling and his small band of Confederates held off a 1,500-man Union force at the Battle of Sabine Pass, a failed Northern invasion that resulted in two sunken Union gunboats and the retreat of the invading Yankee fleet.[16]

The second Confederate monument in Houston, the *Spirit of the Confederacy*, was commissioned by the Robert E. Lee Chapter of the UDC and portrays an angelic symbol of courage and resignation. Sculpted by Italian American artist Louis Amateis, the twelve-foot-tall allegorical figure perched on a base of Texas red granite dominates a small rise at Sam Houston Park.[17]

In January 1908, an estimated 5,000 citizens assembled on the anniversary of Robert E. Lee's birthday to witness the unveiling of the statue to the "heroes of the South" carved by the Yankee sculptor. The monument cost $7,500 and the Daughters spent more than nine years trying to raise the necessary funds. The ceremony celebrating the memorial's completion mimicked most others, with speeches and music, but one newspaper reporter, caught in the excitement of the event, wrote with great feeling about the children's chorus. Hundreds of school children gathered around the monument and sang "America," under the direction of their instructor. Soon thousands of adults joined in and "upon the stillness of the air there came the wave of human voice in patriotic song."[18]

Orange, Orange County

Orange is on Interstate 10 and U.S. Highway 90 at the junction of the Sabine River and the Gulf Intercoastal Waterway. The monument is at Evergreen Cemetery on Jackson and Border Streets.

Local schoolchildren collected pennies, and with the help of the W. P. Lane Camp, UCV, and the John Pelham Chapter of the UDC, erected a memorial to the five "unknown Confederate dead" buried in Evergreen Cemetery. According to early UDC records, the men died of illness in a camp for paroled Texans (near the Sabine River), waiting for

SACRED MEMORIES

their release from the Confederate Army. The dead men's names were lost in the confusion of the war's ending. Such camps were rife with illness, particularly measles and dysentery, and far more Civil War soldiers died of disease than from battle wounds during the war.[19]

The Daughters placed the monument in the cemetery during the 1910s at a cost of $250. The stone is a six-foot granite shaft engraved with the simple phrase, "unknown Confederate dead." Each year descendents of Confederate veterans place wreaths of flowers on the stone to honor the men.[20]

The Pelham Chapter of the UDC was organized in 1900 and remains active. It was named in honor of Maj. John Pelham, a young artillery officer who served with Gen. "Stonewall" Thomas Jackson and died at the Battle of Kelley's Ford, Virginia, in 1863. Over the years, the Pelham Chapter has placed countless markers on the graves of Confederate veterans to honor the men's service in the Southern army.[21]

Wharton, Wharton County

Wharton lies on the east bank of the lower Colorado River, forty-five miles from the Gulf of Mexico, south of U.S. Highway 59. The monument is on the corner of Milam (State Highway 60) and Houston streets, on the courthouse lawn.

The J. E. B. Stuart Chapter of the UDC erected the memorial for local veterans of the Buchel Camp, UCV. The memorial's gray granite shaft bears the names of sixty-eight Confederate veterans from Wharton County. Mary R. Bolton organized the local UDC chapter in 1897. She remained an active clubwoman all her life, chartering other clubs in Wharton, including the Woman's Missionary Society and the Woman's Christian Temperance Union. Before her death, she claimed to be the oldest living graduate of Baylor University, having graduated in 1867.[22]

Appendix:
TABLE OF MONUMENTS

City	County	Year Dedicated	Creator/Designer*	Location	Type
Amarillo	Potter	1931	H. A. Whitacre, N.Y.	Ellwood Park	Confederate
Alvin	Brazoria	1924	unknown	Confederate Cemetery	Confederate
Austin	Travis	1902	Frank Teich	Texas State Capitol grounds	Confederate
		1905	Elisabet Ney	Texas State Cemetery	Confederate
		1907	Louis Amateis	Texas State Capitol grounds	Confederate
		1910	Pompeo Coppini	Texas State Capitol grounds	Confederate
		1933	Pompeo Coppini	South Mall, UT. campus	Confederate
Bastrop	Bastrop	1910	unknown	Courthouse lawn	Confederate
Bay City	Matagorda	1913	unknown	7th St. and Ave. F	Confederate
Belton	Bell	1916	unknown	Courthouse lawn	Confederate
Beaumont	Jefferson	1913	McNeel Marble Co., Ga.	Weiss Park	Confederate
Bonham	Fannin	1905	Bonham Marble Works	Courthouse lawn	Confederate

City	County	Year Dedicated	Creator/Designer*	Location	Type
Brownsville	Cameron	1926	unknown	International Blvd.	Confederate
Bryan	Brazos	1900	unknown	City Cemetery	Confederate
Clarksville	Red River	c. 1920	unknown	Downtown City Square	Confederate
Cleburne	Johnson	1917	unknown	Cleburne Memorial Cemetery	Confederate
College Station	Brazos	1919	unknown	Academic Bldg., TAMU	Confederate
Comfort	Kendall	1866	unknown	High St.	Union
Corpus Christi	Nueces	1915	Pompeo Coppini	Broadway Bluff e Balustrad	Confederate
Corsicana	Navarro	1908	Bureau Bros. Bronze Founders, Philadelphia, Penn.	Courthouse lawn	Confederate
Dallas	Dallas	1897	Frank Teich	Dallas Convention Center	Confederate
		1936	Alexander Phimister Proctor	Lee Park	Confederate
		1936	Laurence Tenney Stevens	Fair Park, Centennial Bldg.	Confederate
		1901	unknown	Greenwood Cemetery	Confederate
Denison	Grayson	1906	Denison Marble Works	Fairview Cemetery	Union
Denton	Denton	1918	unknown	Courthouse lawn	Confederate
El Paso	El Paso	1919	unknown	Evergreen Cemetery	Confederate
Ennis	Ellis	1906	unknown	Myrtle Cemetery	Confederate
Farmersville	Collin	1917	unknown	City Park	Confederate
Fort Worth	Tarrant	1939	unknown	Oakwood Cemetery	Confederate
Gainesville	Cook	1908	unknown	Courthouse lawn	Confederate
		1908	unknown	Leonard Park	Confederate

City	County	Year Dedicated	Creator/Designer*	Location	Type
Galveston	Galveston	1911	unknown	Courthouse lawn	Confederate
		Unknown	unknown	Episcopal Cemetery	Confederate
Georgetown	Williamson	1916	McNeel Marble Co., Ga.	Courthouse lawn	Confederate
Granbury	Hood	1908	Youngblood Monument Co., Waxahachie	Courthouse lawn	Confederate
Greenville	Hunt	1926	No. Tex. Marble and Granite Works	Stanford and King Sts.	Confederate
Gonzales	Gonzales	1909	Frank Teich	St. Louis and Paul Sts.	Confederate
Hillsboro	Hill	1925	Hillsboro Monument Works Co.	Courthouse lawn	Confederate
Houston	Harris	1905	Frank Teich	Sam Houston Park	Confederate
		1908	Louis Amateis	Hermann Park	Confederate
Huntsville	Walker	1956	unknown	Courthouse lawn	Confederate
Jefferson	Marion	1907	Frank Teich	Courthouse lawn	Confederate
Kaufman	Kaufman	1911	Morris Bros.	Courthouse lawn	Confederate
Linden	Cass	1903	unknown	Courthouse lawn	Confederate
Livingston	Polk	1900	unknown	Courthouse lawn	Confederate
Longview	Gregg	1911	Frank Teich	Courthouse lawn	Confederate
Llano	Llano	1916	James K. Finlay & Sons	Courthouse lawn	Confederate
Lubbock	Lubbock	Unknown	unknown	Courthouse lawn	Confederate
Marlin	Falls	1925	unknown	Courthouse lawn	Confederate
Marshall	Harrison	1906	Frank Teich	Old Courthouse lawn	Confederate
		1908	unknown	City cemetery	Confederate
Memphis	Hall	1924	Backus Monument Co., Vernon	Courthouse lawn	Confederate
Mount Pleasant	Titus	c. 1911	unknown	Courthouse lawn	Confederate
New Braunfels	Comal	1935	unknown	E. San Antonio and Seguin Aves,	Union & Confederate

City	County	Year Dedicated	Creator/Designer*	Location	Type
Orange	Orange	c. 1910	unknown	Evergreen Cemetery	Confederate
Palestine	Anderson	1911	Pompeo Coppini	Reagan Park	Confederate
Paris	Lamar	1904	Pompeo Coppini	Courthouse lawn	Confederate
Rusk	Cherokee	1907	unknown	Courthouse lawn	Confederate
San Antonio	Bexar	1900	Frank Teich	Travis Park	Confederate
Scottsville	Harrison	1915	Frank Teich	Scottsville Cemetery	Confederate
Sherman	Grayson	1897	E. T. Bergen and Co., Ft. Worth	Courthouse lawn	Confederate
Temple	Bell	1910	unknown	Hillcrest Cemetery	Confederate
Texarkana	Bowie	1917	Albert Weiblem Marble and Granite Co., New Orleans	UDC Park	Confederate women
Tyler	Smith	1909	Morris Bros. Marble Works, Tyler	Oakwood Cemetery	Confederate
Vernon	Wilbarger	1916	Backus Monument Co., Vernon	Courthouse lawn	Confederate
Victoria	Victoria	1912	Pompeo Coppini	De Leon Plaza	Confederate
Waco	McClellan	1893	unknown	Oakwood Cemetery	Confederate
Waxahachie	Ellis	1912	Youngblood Monument Co., Waxahachie	Courthouse lawn	Confederate
Wharton	Wharton	Unknown	unknown	Courthouse lawn	Confederate
Wichita Falls	Wichita	1934	unknown	W. I. Memorial Auditorium	Confederate

* Designed in Texas unless otherwise indicated.

NOTES

Introduction

[1] United Daughters of the Confederacy, Dixie Chapter 35, *One Hundred Years of Caring, 1896–1996*, in vertical file, "Grayson County: Civil War, Confederacy, etc.," Lucas Collection (Sherman Public Library, Sherman, Tex.), 12 (quotation).

[2] Mattie Davis Lucas, *A History of Grayson County, Texas* (Sherman, Tex.: Scruggs Printing Co., 1948), 202; *Dallas Morning News*, Apr. 22, 1897. Sherman claims to have erected the first monument in Texas, but this is not true. Waco unveiled a monument on May 2, 1893 (Decoration Day), in its city cemetery. The Sherman monument is the first Confederate monument erected on a courthouse lawn. For a contemporary reaction to Sherman's claims, see the letter in the *Confederate Veteran* from Dr. J. C. J. King, *Confederate Veteran*, 5 (July, 1897), 388. For a photograph of the Waco monument, see Ralph W. Widner Jr., *Confederate Monuments: Enduring Symbols of the South and the War Between the States* (Washington, D.C.: Andromeda Association, 1982), 231.

[3] The sixty-eight large public monuments discussed in this text represent memorials of significant scale and do not include tablets on buildings or highway intersections. All of these monuments are located in Texas, though there are Civil War memorials erected to and by Texans in other states, particularly on preserved battlefields. For example, Texans erected a monument at the Raymond Civil War Battlefield in Raymond, Mississippi, on May 4, 2002, memorializing the Texans who fought there in the Vicksburg Campaign. See Clione B. Rochat, "First Monument Dedicated at Raymond Civil War Battlefield," <http://battleofraymond.org/history/dedication.htm> [Accessed Apr. 6, 2006]. For information on monuments in states other than Texas, see Kathryn A. Jacob, *Testament to Union: Civil War Monuments in Washington, D.C.* (Baltimore: Johns Hopkins University Press, 1998); Susan C. Soderberg, *Lest We Forget: A Guide to Civil War Monuments in Maryland* (Shippensburg, Penn.: White Mane Publishing, 1995); and Charles Russell Logan, *"Something So Dim It Must Be Holy": Civil War Commemorative Sculpture in Arkansas, 1886–1937* (Little Rock: Arkansas Historic Preservation Program, [n.d.]).

[4] For more information see, Kristin Ann Hass, *Carried to the War: American Memory and the Vietnam Veterans' Memorial* (Berkeley: University of California Press, 1998).

[5] For examples of public art as social power and markers of social meaning, see Sanford Levinson, *Written in Stone: Public Monuments in Changing Societies* (Durham, N.C.: Duke University Press, 1998), 38–43; John Bodnar, *Remaking America: Public Memory, Commemoration, and Patriotism in the Twentieth Century* (Princeton, N. J.: Princeton University Press, 1992); Michael Kammen, *Mystic Chords of Memory: the Transformation of Tradition in American Culture* (New York: Alfred A. Knopf, 1991); and Thomas J. Brown, *The Public Art of Civil War Commemoration: A Brief History with Documents* (Boston: Bedford/St. Martin's, 2004).

[6] For information on the collectivization of memory, see David Paul Nord, "The Uses of Memory: An Introduction," *The Journal of American History*, 85 (Sep., 1988), 409–410.

[7] Randolph B. Campbell, *Gone to Texas: A History of the Lone Star State* (New York: Oxford University Press), 241–246.

[8] Campbell, *Gone to Texas*, 241–246 (quotations).

[9] Rollin G. Osterweis, *The Myth of the Lost Cause, 1865–1900* (Hamden, Conn.: Archon Books, 1973), x, 11; Thomas L. Connelly and Barbara C. Bellows, *God and General Longstreet* (Baton Rouge: Louisiana State University Press, 1982), 2; Gaines M. Foster, *Ghosts of the Confederacy: Defeat, The Lost Cause, and the Emergence of the New South* (New York: Oxford University Press, 1987), 125; Charles Reagan Wilson, *Baptized in Blood: The Religion of the Lost Cause, 1865–1920* (Athens: University of Georgia Press, 1983), 11.

[10] For more information about commemoration themes in the North, see Thomas J. Brown, *The Public Art of Civil War Commemoration: A Brief History with Documents* (Boston: Bedford/St. Martin's, 2004), 7–9; and Connecticut Historical Society, "Civil War Monuments of Connecticut," <www.chs.org/ransom/introd.htm> [Accessed May 4, 2006]. For information on the monument in Comfort, see Carol Little, *A Comprehensive Guide to Outdoor Sculpture in Texas* (Austin: University of Texas Press, 1996), 118; and *Dallas Morning News*, Jan. 12, 1986. For information concerning the statue in Denison, see Little, *Outdoor Sculpture*, 191. For information about the New Braunfels monument, see "Missing Piece of History to be Replaced," *New Braunfels Herald*, Mar. 15, 1935, in vertical file, "New Braunfels: History—Historical Landmarks," (New Braunfels Public Library, New Braunfels, Tex.); and Little, *Outdoor Sculpture*, 342.

[11] Only five percent of known Union inscriptions on monuments refer explicitly to the abolition of slavery as a war achievement. Both Northerners and Southerners chose to ignore the broader issue of slavery and abolition in public works of art. For more information, see Brown, *Public Art*, 37–39; and "Civil War Monuments Provide a Glimpse into History," *University Times* (University of Pittsburgh), Oct. 23, 1997, <www.pitt.edu/utimes/issues/30/102397/21.html> [Accessed May 4, 2006]. For more on faithful slaves monuments, see Paul Shackel, *Memory in Black*

and White: Race, Commemoration, and the Post-bellum Landscape (Lanham, Md.: Rowman & Littlefield, 2003), 87.

[12] John J. Winberry, "'Lest We Forget': The Confederate Monument and the Southern Townscape," *Southeastern Geographer*, 23 (Nov., 1983): 107–121.

[13] William W. White, *The Confederate Veteran* (Tuscaloosa, Ala.: Confederate Publishing, 1962); *Confederate Soldier*, 1 (Oct., 1901), 6; *Confederate Veteran*, 5 (Oct., 1897), 498. For more on Southern women erecting monuments, see Cynthia Mills and Pamela H. Simpson (eds.), *Monuments to the Lost Cause: Women, Art, and the Landscapes of Southern Memory* (Knoxville: University of Tennessee Press, 2003).

[14] *Dallas Morning News*, Apr. 22, 1897; *Sherman Daily Register*, Apr. 3, 1896.

[15] *Confederate Soldier*, 1 (Oct., 1901), 13–14 (1st quotation); *Houston Chronicle*, June 13, 1909 (2nd quotation).

[16] *Proceedings of the Fifth Annual Convention of the Texas Division, United Daughters of the Confederacy* (Ennis, Tex.: Hal Marchbanks, Printer, 1900), 7; *Southern Tribute*, 1 (Apr./May, 1898), 307 (2nd quotation). For sources that discuss the UDC and monument erections, see Melody Kubassek, "Ask Us Not to Forget: The Lost Cause in Natchez, Mississippi," *Southern Studies*, 3 (Fall 1992), 155–170; and Foster, *Ghosts of the Confederacy*, 129.

[17] *Proceedings of the Twelfth Annual Convention of the Texas Division, United Daughters of the Confederacy* (Weatherford, Tex.: Herold Publishing Co., 1908), 28; "U.D.C.," *The Southern Tribute: A Monthly Magazine Devoted to the Daughters of the Confederacy*, 1 (Apr./May, 1898), 297; C. W. Raines, *Yearbook for Texas, 1901* (Austin: Gammel Book Co. Publishers, 1902), 127 (quotations). Mae Wynne McFarland spoke about the "type" of member preferred in her "President's Message" in the 1940s, "No project is more important to the Society than increase in membership—but careful increase. To secure members for the sole purpose of adding numbers would be a fatal error. . . . Never deny membership to a worthy woman seeking it . . . but choose carefully those whom you invite to join. We must value our own membership so highly that we cannot cheapen it by quantity at the expense of quality." See "President's Message," 2, Box 17, Folder 4, McFarland Papers, Thomason Room, Sam Houston State University, Huntsville, Tex.

[18] *The Confederate Daughter*, 1 (June, 1900), 8.

[19] *Texas Division Chapter Histories* (Austin: UDC, Chapter 105, Albert Sidney Johnston, 1990), 8; UDC, *Minutes of the Second Annual Convention of the Texas Division of the United Daughters of the Confederacy* (Galveston: Clarke and Coats, 1898), 11–12 (quotations); *Confederate Soldier and Daughter*, 1 (Feb., 1902), 17–18.

[20] C. W. Raines, *Yearbook for Texas, 1901* (Austin: Gammel Book Co., 1902), 129, in Box 82, Folder 1901, Robertson Colony Collection—Ella Fulmore Harlee Collection (Special Collections, University of Texas at Arlington); *Confederate Veteran*, 10 (Jan., 1902), 10; *Confederate Soldier and Daughter*, 1 (Feb., 1902), 17–18 (quotation).

[21] *Confederate Soldier and Daughter*, 1 (Feb., 1902), 18.

[22] *Dallas Morning News*, June 4, 1911, in vertical file, "Confederate Monument" (Longview Public Library, Longview, Tex.); Kelly McMichael Stott, "The Lost Cause in Dallas, Texas, 1894–1897," *Legacies*, 12 (Spring 2000), 4–12.

[23] *The Confederate Daughter*, 1 (July, 1900), 113.

[24] *Dallas Morning News*, Apr., 28, 1897 (quotation); *Dallas Times Herald*, Apr., 28, 1897; unidentified newspaper clipping in scrapbook, Katie Cabell Currie Muse Papers (Dallas Historical Society, Dallas, Tex.); Stott, "The Lost Cause in Dallas, Texas," 4–12; Wilburn Oatman, *Llano: Gem of the Hill Country. A History of Llano County, Texas* (Llano, Tex: Pioneer Book Publishers, 1970), 115.

[25] "Teich, Frank," *Handbook of Texas Online, www.tsha.utexas.edu/handbook/online/articles/TT/fte5.html* [Accessed May 18, 2006]; File 2, Notebooks 111, 128, and 172, Coppini-Tauch Papers (Center for American History, University of Texas at Austin; cited hereafter as CAH).

[26] File 2, Notebook 111, Coppini-Tauch Papers.

[27] File 2, Notebook 111, Coppini-Tauch Papers.

[28] File 2, Notebook 111, Coppini-Tauch Papers.

[29] File 2, Notebook 111, Coppini-Tauch Papers.

[30] Pompeo Coppini to Mrs. W. P. Lane, Apr. 18, 1921, Box 6, Folder 20, Julia Jackson UDC Chapter Papers (Fort Worth Public Library, Fort Worth, Tex.) (quotations).

[31] For more information on the City Beautiful movement, see William H. Watson, *The City Beautiful Movement* (Baltimore: Johns Hopkins University Press, 1989).

[32] Jeanne Madeline Weimann, *The Fair Women* (Chicago: Academy Chicago, 1981), 270 (quotation); *Dallas Morning News*, Oct. 27, 1893. Some future UDC members attended and played leading roles at the Woman's Congress. These included, for example, Mrs. J. C. Terrell of Fort Worth's Woman's Wednesday Club, who was elected to serve on the Congress's executive board and in 1897 was elected fourth vice president of the Texas UDC. For a summary of the influence of the Woman's Congress on club life in Texas, see Stella L. Christian (ed.), *The History of the Texas Federation of Women's Clubs* (Houston: Dealy-Adey-Elgin Co., 1919), 5–9.

[33] Stott, "The Lost Cause in Dallas," 9; *Dallas Morning News*, June 26, 1896. The Columbian Exposition inspired other organizations toward city beautification and a host of women's groups (for example, the Daughters of the American Revolution and the Daughters of the Republic of Texas) attempted to erect monuments in Texas during this period. For more on the public art throughout the state, see Little, *Outdoor Sculpture*.

[34] "Nueces, Battle of the," *Handbook of Texas Online*, <http://www.tshaonline.org/handbook/online/articles/NN/qfn1.html> [Accessed May 18, 2006].

[35] Letter to editor from Dr. J. C. J. King, *Confederate Veteran*, 5 (July,1897), 388; Widner, *Confederate Monuments*, 231.

[36] Wilson, *Baptized in Blood*, 18; John A. Simpson, "Cult of the Lost Cause," *Tennessee Historical Quarterly*, 34 (Winter, 1975), 353; Gaines M. Foster, *Ghosts*

of the Confederacy: Defeat, The Lost Cause, and the Emergence of the New South, 1865–1913 (New York: Oxford University Press, 1987), 158; James M. Mayo, *War Memorials as Political Landscape: The American Experience and Beyond* (New York: Praeger, 1988), 171.

[37] For a discussion of the erection of Confederate monuments in Arkansas, see Logan, *Something so Dim it Must be Holy.*"

[38] The continued creation of Confederate monuments by Texans well into the 1940s calls into question recent interpretations by Walter Buenger in "Texas and the South" and Gregg Cantrell in "The Bones of Stephen F. Austin," both of whom argue that the state had by its centennial celebration in 1936 begun to move culturally away from its Southern heritage, toward a definition of itself as Western, regaling in its revolutionary past and associating historical memory with a cowboy heritage. These interpretations, combined with studies on Civil War memory in the state, need to be examined more closely and offer a rich area for further study. See Walter L. Buenger, "Texas and the South," *Southwestern Historical Quarterly*, 103 (Jan., 2000), 309 and Gregg Cantrell, "The Bones of Stephen F. Austin: History and Memory in Progressive-Era Texas," *Southwestern Historical Quarterly*, 108 (Oct., 2004), 145–180.

Chapter 1: East Texas

[Huntsville]
[1] D'Anne McAdams Crews (ed.), *Huntsville and Walker County, Texas: A Bicentennial History* (Huntsville, Tex.: Sam Houston State University, 1976), 45; Walker County Genealogical Society and Walker County Historical Commission, *Walker County History* (Dallas: Curtis Media Corp., 1986), 850–851; *Huntsville Item*, Mar. 6, 1941, Mar. 13, 1941, June 28, 1956; vertical file, "The Reunion, CSA—Madison County, Texas" (Huntsville Public Library, Huntsville, Tex.).

[Jefferson]
[2] Fred Tarpley, *Jefferson: Riverport to the Southwest* (Austin: Eakin Press, 1983), 204–210.
[3] Tarpley, *Jefferson*, 204–210; Mrs. Arch McKay and Mrs. H.A. Spelling, (eds.), *A History of Jefferson Marion County, Texas, 1836–1936* (Jefferson, Tex.: [n.p.], 1936), 40–41.
[4] Tarpley, *Jefferson*, 208 (1st and 2nd quotations).
[5] *Marshall Evening Messenger*, Jan. 19, 1906 (quotation).
[6] Tarpley, *Jefferson*, 209.
[7] Tarpley, *Jefferson*, 204–205, 209–210 (quotation on p. 205).
[8] Tarpley, *Jefferson*, 209.
[Linden]
[9] *Cass County Sun*, July 7, 9, 1903 (quote), Oct. 20, 29, 1903, Nov. 3, 10, 1903.
[10] *Cass County Sun*, July 7, 9, 1903 (quote); Sue Morris Lazra to Kelly McMichael, Mar. 19, 2003, interview (transcript in possession of author).
[11] Lazra to McMichael, Mar. 19, 2003.
[12] Lazra to McMichael, Mar.19, 2003 (transcript in possession of authors); *Mar-*

shall News Messenger, Nov. 10, 1963.

[Livingston]

13 Wanda Bobinger to Kelly McMichael, Nov. 12, 2001, interview (notes in possession of author).

14 Bobinger to McMichael, Nov 12, 2001 (interview).

15 Bobinger to McMichael, Nov 12, 2001 (interview).

[Longview]

16 *Dallas Morning News*, June 4, 1911 (quote); *Longview Times Clarion*, June 8, 16, 23, 1911; Viola Cobb Bivins, *Echoes of the Confederacy* (Dallas: Barks and Upshaw & Co., 1951), 118.

17 *Dallas Morning News*, June 4, 1911 (quote).

18 *Dallas Morning News*, June 4, 1911.

19 *Longview Morning Journal*, May 3, 1970.

20 Vertical file, "Courthouses—Gregg County, Texas" (Longview Public Library, Longview, Tex.); Vertical file, "Confederate Museum—Gregg County, Texas" (Longview Public Library, Longview, Tex.).

[Marshall]

21 *Marshall Evening Messenger*, Jan. 19, 1906 (quote).

22 Ledger book, Marshall Chapter of the UDC, 1907 (Marshall Historical Society Museum, Marshall, Tex.).

23 Quotation inscribed on monument.

24 Vertical file, "Confederate Monument" (Marshall Historical Society Museum, Marshall, Tex.).

25 "Confederate Monument."

26 "Confederate Monument," *Marshall News Messenger*, June 3, 1947.

[Mount Pleasant]

27 Russell Traylor, *History of Titus County, Texas, Containing Biographical Sketches of Many Noted Characters* (Waco: W. M. Morrison, 1965), 187–190.

28 Traylor, *History of Titus County, Texas*, 189.

29 Traylor, *History of Titus County, Texas*, 189.

[Palestine]

30 Carl L. Avera, *Centennial Notebook: a Collage of Reminiscences of Palestine's First Century* (Palestine, Tex.: Royale National Bank, 1976).

31 Pompeo Coppini, *From Dawn to Sunset* (San Antonio: Naylor Co., 1949), 198.

Carl L. Avera, *Wind Swept Land* (San Antonio: Naylor Co., 1964), 74; *Confederate Veteran*, 13 (May, 1905), 207.

32 Little, *Outdoor Sculpture*, 350.

33 Mary Kate Hunter, notebooks, vol. I (Palestine Public Library, Palestine, Tex.), 38–64.

34 *Palestine Herald-Press*, June 28, 1967; Lizzie Langenkemp to Kelly McMichael, July 11, 1999, interview (notes in possession of author).

[Rusk]

35 *Confederate Veteran*, 16 (Mar., 1908), 103.

³⁶ Quotation on monument.

³⁷ Jack Moore, *The Great Jacksonville Circus Fight and Other Cherokee County Stories* (Jacksonville, Tex: privately printed, 1971), 36, 38.

[Scottsville]

³⁸ Little, *Outdoor Sculpture*, 411.

³⁹ Little, *Outdoor Sculpture*, 411.

⁴⁰ Little, *Outdoor Sculpture*, 411.

[Texarkana]

⁴¹ Lela McLure "Captain Rosborough and the Confederate Memorial," A Civic Project of the Texarkana Chapter 568, UDC (n.p., n.d.), 1–5.

⁴² Little, *Outdoor Sculpture*, 422; *Confederate Veteran*, 26 (July, 1918), 278; *United Daughters of the Confederacy Magazine*, 24 (July, 1961), 2.

⁴³ Quotation on monument.

[Tyler]

⁴⁴ Little, *Outdoor Sculpture*, 422; *Tyler Semi-Weekly Courier Times*, July 10, 1909 (quotation).

⁴⁵ Little, *Outdoor Sculpture*, 422; *Tyler Courier-Times Telegraph*, June 2, 1963; Vertical file, "UDC" (Tyler Public Library, Tyler, Tex.).

⁴⁶ *Tyler Semi-Weekly Courier Times*, July 10, 1909.

Chapter 2: North Texas

[Bonham]

¹ *Fannin County Favorite*, July 13 (quote), 20, 21, 26, and 27, 1905.

² *Fannin County Favorite*, July 13, 1905.

³ *Confederate Veteran*, 17 (May, 1909), 206–207.

[Clarksville]

⁴ Martha Sue Stroud, *Gateway to Texas: History of Red River County* (Austin: Nortex Press, 1997), 38–39; Little, *Outdoor Sculpture*, 113.

⁵ *The Clarksville Times*, Nov. 4, 1941.

[Denison]

⁶ Little, *Outdoor Sculpture*, 191.

⁷ Little, *Outdoor Sculpture*, 191.

⁸ Little, *Outdoor Sculpture*, 191.

[Denton]

⁹ *Denton Record-Chronicle*, June 3, 1918.

¹⁰ *Dallas Morning News*, July 20, 1999; *Denton Record-Chronicle*, Sep. 17, 2000 (quote).

[Gainesville]

¹¹ First two quotations are from the inscription on the monument; *Confederate Veteran*, 16 (Aug., 1908), 377 (third quote).

¹² Vertical file, "History of Cook County" (Cook County Library, Gainesville, Tex.). For more on the Great Hanging, see Richard McCaslin, *Tainted Breeze: The Great Hanging at Gainesville, Texas, 1862* (Baton Rouge: Louisiana State University Press, 1997).

[Paris]

13 Coppini-Tauch Papers, File 2, notebook, 128–129 (CAH).

14 Coppini-Tauch Papers, File 2, notebook, 128–129 (CAH); Coppini-Tauch Papers, scrapbook (CAH) (quote); *Confederate Veteran*, 12 (Mar., 1904), 120; Elizabeth Booth and Tony Booth, *Evergreen Cemetery Book* (n.p., n.d.), 71–72.

15 *Paris Farmers Advocate*, Oct. 29, 1903.

16 Little, *Outdoor Sculpture*, 352.

[Sherman]

17 Vertical file, "Grayson County: Civil War, confederacy, etc." (Lucas Collection, Sherman Public Library, Sherman, Tex.); Little, *Outdoor Sculpture*, 412.

18 "A Brief Sketch of Dixie Chapter, UDC, No. 35," in vertical file, "Grayson County: Civil War, confederacy, etc." (Lucas Collection, Sherman Public Library, Sherman, Tex.).

19 *Dallas Morning News*, Apr. 22, 1897.

20 *Dallas Morning News*, Apr. 22, 1897. (quote); *Sherman Democrat*, July 4, 1976, Oct. 28, 1936; Little, *Outdoor Sculpture*, 412; Mattie Davis Lucas, *A History of Grayson County, Texas* (Sherman, Tex: Scruggs Printing Co., 1948), 202–203.

Chapter 3: North Central Texas

[Cleburne]

1 *Confederate Veteran*, 5 (July, 1897), 388.

2 Sandra Osborne, to Kelly McMichael, Mar. 14, 2003 (original in possession of the author).

[Corsicana]

3 *Confederate Veteran*, 16 (May, 1908), 178, 210–211; Little, *Outdoor Sculpture*, 129.

4 Wyvonne Putman (comp.), *Navarro County History: Public Buildings, Historical Events, and Early Businesses* (Quanah, Tex: Nortex Press, 1975), V, 298; *Confederate Veteran*, 12 (Jan., 1904), 120 (quotations).

[Dallas]

5 Little, *Outdoor Sculpture*, 161–165; *Confederate Veteran*, 4 (Jan., 1896), 22; *Confederate Veteran*, 4 (July 1896), 202–203; Katie Cabell Currie Muse Papers (Dallas Historical Society, Dallas, Tex.).

6 *Confederate Veteran*, 3 (Oct., 1895), 307; *Dallas Morning News*, Apr. 29, 30, 1897(quote); *Confederate Veteran*, 6 (July 1898); *Dallas Morning News*, Aug. 4, 1894, May 24, 1896, June 26, 1896, Aug. 4, 1992, Oct. 13, 1997, Dec. 7, 1988.

7 *Dallas Morning News*, Dec. 7, 1988; Little, *Outdoor Sculpture*, 161–165 (quote)

8 Little, *Outdoor Sculpture*, 162.

9 Little, *Outdoor Sculpture*, 163; *Dallas Morning News*, Dec. 7, 1988.

10 Little, *Outdoor Sculpture*, 164.

[Ennis]

11 Quotation on the monument; Vertical file, "Katie Daffan" (Ennis Public Library, Ennis, Tex.).

[12] Vertical file, "Katie Daffan."

[Farmersville]

[13] Pansy Hundley to Kelly McMichael, Dec. 19, 2001 (original in possession of the author) ;
Vertical file, "Farmersville, Tex., Nov. 11, 1912" (Charles J. Rike Memorial Library, Farmersville, Tex.)

[Fort Worth]

[14] Pompeo Coppini to Julia Jackson Chapter, July 8, 1921, Julia Jackson Chapter Records, UDC, Box 6: 20 (Fort Worth Public Library, Fort Worth, Tex.).

[15] Pompeo Coppini to Julia Jackson Chapter. Gutzon Borglum's well-known sculptures include the presidential monument at Mount Rushmore in South Dakota and Stone Mountain monument of Confederate leaders in Georgia. Learn more about Borglum in Rex Alan Smith, *The Carving of Mount Rushmore* (New York: Abbeville Press, 1985)

[16] Little, *Outdoor Sculpture*, 216.

[17] Little, *Outdoor Sculpture*, 216.

[Granbury]

[18] Little, *Outdoor Sculpture*, 240.

[19] *Granbury News*, July 2, 1908, Jan. 24, 1914.

[20] *Granbury News*, Jan. 24, 1914.

[Greenville]

[21] Little, *Outdoor Sculpture*, 241; UDC, Greenville Chapter Minute Book, 1924–1928 (W. Walworth Harrison Public Library, Greenville, Tex.).

[22] Greenville Chapter Minute Book, 1924–1928 (quotes); *Greenville Messenger*, Apr. 8, 1926; *Greenville Morning Herald*, June 8, 1926.

[Hillsboro]

[23] *Hillsboro Mirror*, July 29, 1925; Little, *Outdoor Sculpture*, 246.

[24] Harold B. Simpson, *Hill County (Texas) Trilogy* (Hillsboro, Tex.: Hill College Press, 1986), 71–84.

[25] *Hillsboro Mirror*, July 29, 1925.

[Kaufman]

[26] *Kaufman Sun*, Sep. 18, 1908; Horace P. Flatt, Kaufman County Historical Commission, to Kelly McMichael, Jan. 25, 2002 (letter in possession of the author).

[27] *Kaufman Sun*, Sept. 18, 1908 (quote).

[28] *Kaufman Sun*, Sep. 18, 1908; Quotation from monument.

[29] Little, *Outdoor Sculpture*, 308; *Kaufman Herald*, Apr. 26, 1956; *Terrell Daily Tribune*, Aug. 28, 1956.

[30] Little, *Outdoor Sculpture*, 308.

[Waxahachie]

[31] Vertical files, "History—Waxahachie," Folder 3, and "Ellis County—Courthouse" (Nicholas P. Sims Public Library, Waxahachie, Tex.).

[32] "History—Waxahachie."

[33] "History—Waxahachie."

[34] "History—Waxahachie."

Chapter 4: Central Texas

[Austin]

[1] *United Daughters of the Confederacy, Texas Division Chapter Histories* (Austin: UDC Chapter 105, Albert Sidney Johnston, 1990), 8; *Minutes of the Second Annual Convention of the Texas Division of the United Daughters of the Confederacy* (Galveston: Clarke and Coats, 1898), 11–12; (quotation); *Confederate Veteran*, 10 (Jan, 1902), 10.

[2] *United Daughters of the Confederacy, Texas Division Chapter Histories*, 8 (quotation).

[3] *Confederate Soldier and Daughter*, 1 (Feb. 1902), 17–18.

[4] C. W. Raines, *Yearbook for Texas, 1901* (Austin: Gammel Book Co., 1902), 129, in Robertson Colony Collection—Ella Fulmore Harlee Collection, Box 82, Folder 1901, Special Collections (University of Texas at Arlington Library, Arlington, Tex.).

[5] *Confederate Veteran*, 18 (Dec, 1910), 564.

[6] Coppini-Tauch Papers, File 2, notebook, 130 (CAH).

[7] *Confederate Veteran*, 18 (Dec, 1910), 564; Coppini-Tauch Papers, File 2, notebook, 130 (CAH) (quotation).

[8] *United Daughters of the Confederacy, Texas Division Chapter Histories*, 15.

[9] *United Daughters of the Confederacy, Texas Division Chapter Histories*, 15.

[10] *Confederate Veteran*, 18 (Dec, 1910), 564 (quotation).

[11] *Confederate Veteran* 20 (Dec, 1912), 592; Vertical file, "Katie Cabell Muse Chapter, Austin Chapter 2166—Yearbook, 1959-1960" (Austin History Center, Austin, Tex.).

[12] Vertical file, "Katie Cabell Muse Chapter, Austin Chapter 2166—Yearbook, 1959–1960" (Austin History Center, Austin, Tex.); Coppini-Tauch Papers, File 2, notebook, 142 (CAH) (quotation).

[13] Coppini-Tauch Papers, File 2, notebook, 142 (CAH) (quotation).

[14] Coppini-Tauch Papers, File 2, notebook, 142.

[Bastrop]

[15] *Confederate Veteran*, 19 (Jan. 1911), 1.

[16] Ibid.

[Belton]

[17] Little, *Outdoor Sculpture*, 96; Emily W. Countess, "History Bell County Chapter 101—U.D.C., 1896–1982," Genealogy Collection (Belton City Library, Belton, Tex.), 1–4; Bertha Atkinson, *History of Bell County, Texas* (Belton, Tex.: Bell County Historical Society, 1970), 114–115.

[18] Emily W. Countess, "History Bell County Chapter 101—U.D.C., 1896–1982," Genealogy Collection (Belton City Library, Belton, Tex.), 1–4; Atkinson, *History of Bell County*, 114–115.

[Bryan]

[19] *Confederate Veteran*, 8 (Aug., 1900), 370.

[College Station]
20 Little, *Outdoor Sculpture*, 114.
21 "Ross, Lawrence Sullivan," *The Handbook of Texas Online*, <www.tsha. utexas.edu/handbook/online/articles/view/RR/fro81.html> [Accessed Nov. 2, 2002].
22 "Ross, Lawrence Sullivan."
23 "Ross, Lawrence Sullivan."
[Georgetown]
24 Little, *Outdoor Sculpture*, 235.
25 Little, *Outdoor Sculpture*, 235.
[Llano]
26 James E. Ferguson, "Speech of Governor James E. Ferguson at the Unveiling of a Confederate Monument in Llano, Texas," Feb. 22, 1916, (Texas States Archives, Austin, Tex.); Wilburn Oatman, *Llano: Gem of the Hill Country, A History of Llano County, Texas* (Hereford, Tex.: Pioneer Book Publishers, 1970), 113–115 (quote).
27 Oatman, *Llano: Gem of the Hill Country*, 113–115.
28 Oatman, *Llano: Gem of the Hill Country*, 113–115; Little, *Outdoor Sculpture*, 315.
[Marlin]
29 Unmarked Newspaper article, Vertical file, "Confederacy" (Memorial Public Library, Marlin, Tex.).
30 Vertical file, "Confederacy."
31 "Marlin, Texas," *Handbook of Texas Online*, <http://www.tshaonline.org/handbook/online/articles/MM/hfm2.html> [Accessed Oct.17, 2008].
[Temple]
32 *Confederate Veteran*, 18 (Sept., 1910), 424; *Confederate Veteran*, 22 (Feb., 1915), 74; For more information on Father Abram J. Ryan see, Father Abram J. Ryan, *Poet of the Confederacy: Selected Poems* (Richmond: Brannon Publishing Co., 1999).
33 Patty Benoit to Kelly McMichael, Mar. 27, 2003, e-mail (printed copy in possession of author).
[Waco]
34 *Waco Evening News*, May 2, 1893; Cemetery Records, Oakwood Cemetery, McLennan County, Tex., Texas Collection (Baylor University Library, Waco. Tex.).
35 *Waco Evening News*, May 2, 1893.
36 *Waco Evening News*, May 2, 1893.

Chapter 5: The Panhandle and West Texas
[Amarillo]
1 *Confederate Veteran*, 39 (July, 1931), 263; Little, *Outdoor Sculpture*, 53.
2 *Confederate Veteran*, 39 (July, 1931).
[El Paso]
3 *El Paso Herald Post*, 1949; *Southwestern Clubwoman*, 5 (July, 1949), 1, 21.

[4] Quotations on monument.

[Lubbock]

[5] "Lubbock, Thomas Saltus," *Handbook of Texas Online*, < http://www.tshaonline.org/handbook/online/articles/LL/flu2.html> [Accessed Oct. 6, 2007] (quotation).

[6] " Lubbock, Thomas Saltus," *Handbook of Texas Online.*

[Memphis]

[7] Little, *Outdoor Sculpture*, 333.

[8] *Memphis Democrat*, Oct. 25, 1923, Mar. 22, 1928, 12 Apr. 12, 1928.

[9] Karen Crisman, "Veteran's Monument, Memphis, Texas," unpublished paper (copy in possession of author).

[10] Crisman, "Veteran's Monument."

[Vernon]

[11] Little, *Outdoor Sculpture*, 430.

[Wichita Falls]

[12] Vertical file, "UDC," Louise Kelly Collection (Wichita County Archives, Wichita Falls, Tex.).

[13] "Scurry, William Read." *Handbook of Texas Online*, < http://www.tshaonline.org/handbook/online/articles/SS/fsc38.html> (Accessed Oct. 6, 2007); *Wichita Daily Times*, Jan. 25 1931, June 4, 1944, June 5, 1950.

[14] *Wichita Falls Times*, Apr. 8, 1969, Apr. 26, 1974; Vertical file, "UDC," Louise Kelly Collection (Wichita County Archives, Wichita Falls, Tex.)

[15] "UDC," Louise Kelly Collection.

Chapter 6: South Texas

[Brownsville]

[1] *Confederate Veteran*, 35 (Nov., 1927), 423; Little, *Outdoor Sculpture*, 118.

[2] "Davis, Jefferson," *Handbook of Texas Online*, <http://www.tshaonline.org/handbook/online/articles/DD/fda42.html> [Accessed Oct. 6, 2007].

[3] Palmito Ranch, Battle of, *The Handbook of Texas Online*, < http://www.tshaonline.org/handbook/online/articles/PP/qfp1.html> [Accessed Oct. 6, 2007].

[Comfort]

[4] "Comfort, TX," *The Handbook of Texas Online*, < http://www.tshaonline.org/handbook/online/articles/CC/hjc16.html> [Accessed Oct. 6, 2007].

[5] "Nueces, Battle of," *The Handbook of Texas Online*, < http://www.tshaonline.org/handbook/online/articles/NN/qfn1.html > [Accessed Oct. 6, 2007].

[6] *Dallas Morning News*, Jan. 12, 1986, July 28, 1996; "Nueces, Battle of," *The Handbook of Texas Online*. For information about the continued friction between Unionists and secessionists in Texas after the war see, Stanley S. McGowen, "Battle or Massacre? The Incident on the Nueces, August 10, 1862," *Southwestern Historical Quarterly* 104 (July, 2000), 65–86.

[7] Little, *Outdoor Sculpture*, 118.

[8] *Dallas Morning News* Jan. 12, 1986; July 28, 1996.

[Corpus Christi]

⁹ Vertical files, "Corpus Christi Monuments," and "Historical Sites" (Corpus Christi Public Library, Corpus Christi, Tex.).

¹⁰ Vertical file, "Monuments, Daughters of the Confederacy memorial," (Corpus Christi Public Library, Corpus Christi, Tex.).

¹¹ John Wright, "Pompeo Coppini and Corpus Christi's First Experiment with Public Art," Dec. 12, 1989, unpublished material (Daughters of Republic of Texas Library, San Antonio, Tex.) (quotes); Frances C. Ranc, "Queen of the Sea," *United Daughters of the Confederacy Magazine* (Dec., 1991) 30.

¹² *Corpus Christi Caller Times*, Jan. 20, 1956 (quote).

¹³ Jan. 30, 1966 (quote); Brochure for Corpus Christi Rededication Ceremony, Apr. 14, 1991 (in possession of the author).

[Gonzales]

¹⁴ *Confederate Veteran*, 18 (July, 1910), 321; Little, *Outdoor Sculpture*, 239.

¹⁵ *San Antonio Daily Express*, Sept. 30, 1909 (quotes).

[New Braunfels]

¹⁶ Little, *Outdoor Sculpture*, 342.

¹⁷ *New Braunfels Herald-Zeitung*, Mar. 15, 1935; Vertical file, "New Braunfels: History—Historical Landmarks" (City of New Braunfels Library, New Braunfels, Tex.).

¹⁸ Vertical file, "New Braunfels: History—Historical Landmarks."

¹⁹ *The Herald-Zeitung Presents Images of New Braunfels, Comal County, Texas*, vol. 1 (New Braunfels: *Herald-Zeitung*, 2002); Lynn Thompson, to Kelly McMichael, Feb. 20, 21, and 26, 2003, e-mail (printed copies in possession of the author); Vertical file, "New Braunfels: History—Historical Landmarks," (quote).

[San Antonio]

²⁰ *San Antonio Daily Express*, Apr. 28 and 29, 1900.

²¹ Vertical file, "Travis Park" (Daughters of the Republic of Texas Library, San Antonio, Tex.).

²² Vertical file, "UDC, B. E. Bee Chapter," (Daughters of the Republic of Texas Library, San Antonio, Tex.); *Confederate Veteran*, 7 (Sept., 1899) (quote), 399; *Confederate Veteran*, 8 (June, 1900), 261.

²³ Little, *Outdoor Sculpture*, 395.

[Victoria]

²⁴ Coppini-Tauch Papers, scrapbook, (pages not numbered), 1908–1915 (CAH), (quotations).

²⁵ *Confederate Veteran*, 19 (Jan., 1912), 13; *Confederate Veteran*, 20 (Sep., 1912), 411; William P. Rogers Chapter 44, *Yearbook*, Special Collections, Archives, (University of Houston–Victoria Library, University of Houston—Victoria College, Victoria, Tex.) *San Antonio Express*, Feb. 19, and 26, 1911.

²⁶ *San Antonio Express*, Feb. 26, 1911; *Confederate Veteran*, 20 (Sep., 1912).

²⁷ *San Antonio Express*, Feb. 19, 1911 (quote).

²⁸ *San Antonio Express*, Feb. 19, 1911.

Chapter 7: Southeast Texas

[Alvin]

1 Jamie Murray to Kelly McMichael, Mar. 29, 2003, e-mail (printed copy in possession of author).

2 Murray to McMichael, Mar. 29, 2003, e-mail.

[Bay City]

3 Little, *Outdoor Sculpture*, 89.

4 Little, *Outdoor Sculpture*, 89.

5 "Fort Esperanza," *The Handbook of Texas Online*, <http://www.tshaonline.org/handbook/online/articles/FF/qcf2.html> [Accessed Oct. 7, 2007].

[Beaumont]

6 *Confederate Veteran*, 21 (Mar, 1913), 126, (quotation).

7 *Confederate Veteran*, 21 (Mar, 1913), 126; Little, *Outdoor Sculpture*, 94.

8 *Confederate Veteran*, 21 (Mar, 1913), 126.

9 *Confederate Veteran*, 21 (Mar, 1913), 126.

10 Little, *Outdoor Sculpture*, 94.

[Galveston]

11 Vertical file, "Monuments in Galveston" (Rosenberg Library, Galveston, Tex.).

12 *Galveston Daily News*, Apr. 22, 1900, Jan. 20, 1906, Jan. 23, 1911 (quote).

13 "Monuments in Galveston".

14 "Monuments in Galveston."

[Houston]

15 *Houston Daily Post*, Mar. 17 and 18, 1905; Little, *Outdoor Sculpture*, 247.

16 *Houston Daily Post*, Mar. 18, 1905.

17 "History of the Robert E. Lee Chapter of the UDC," unpublished manuscript (Houston Public Library, Houston, Tex.).

18 Jan. 19 and 20 (quote), 1908; *Confederate Veteran*, 18 (Feb., 1910), 65; Little, *Outdoor Sculpture*, 272.

[Orange]

19 *The Orange Leader*, Sep. 21, 1980, Nov. 16, 1980; Rhonda Stanley to Kelly McMichael, Mar. 7, 2003 (original in possession of the author).

20 The Orange Leader, Sep. 21, 1980.

21 Rhonda Stanley to Kelly McMichael, Mar. 7, 2003.

[Wharton]

22 *Houston Daily Post*, Mar. 4, 1938; *The Wharton Spectator*, May 28, 1915; Brett A. Glenn to Kelly McMichael, Mar. 28, 2003 (original in possession of author); "Confederate Monument, Wharton County Courthouse" (Wharton County Historical Museum, Wharton, Tex., [n.d].).A

INDEX

Alvin monument, 85
Amarillo monument, 70, 71
Amateis, Louis, 45, 59–60, 90
American Legion, 80
American Legion Auxiliary, 73
American Legion Ladies Auxiliary, 80
American Legion Post 175, 73
American Revolution, 60
Atlanta, Georgia, Confederate monuments in, 17
Austin Confederate Monument, 57, 58–59
Austin monuments, 10–11, 13, 57–62

Backus, G. W., 74
Backus Monument Company, 74
Baldwin, Briscoe G., 63
Bastrop monument, 62
Bay City monument, 85–86
Beaumont monument, 86–87
Bell County Chapter, UDC, 63
Belton monument, 62–63
Bernard E. Bee Chapter, UDC, 81
Bodenheim, G. A., 26
Bodie Park, Longview, 26
Bolton, Mary R., 91
Bonham monument, 35–36
Borglum, Gutzon, 50
Brownsville monument, 76
Bryan monument, 63

Buchel Camp, UCV, 91

cabins, memorial, 68
Call to Arms (monument), 45
Camp Douglas (Union prisoner of war camp), 16
Camp Hood Confederate Veterans, 58
Cass County courthouse, 24, 25
Chamberlain, A. P., 38
Chatham, R. Q., 64
China Spring Camp, UCV, 69
City Beautiful movement, 15–16
City Park, Farmersville, 49
civil rights activists, 38
Civil War: diseases, fatal during, 90–91; reenactments of, 53; veterans, 80; women's participation in, 9
Clark, Mrs. B. C., 67
Clarksville Chapter, UDC, 36
Clarksville monument, 36
Cleburne monument, 44–45
Clousnitzer, Ernest, 80–81
Cochran, Ellana, 79
Cohee, Ira, 80
collective memory, creation and control of, 3–4
College Station monument, 64–66
Colonel Reeves Eleventh Texas Cavalry Camp 349, Sons of Confederate Veterans (SCV), 1

110